OPPORTUNITY IN THE EAST MIDLANDS

East Midlands Economic Planning Council

London: Her Majesty's Stationery Office 1969. Published for the Department of Economic Affairs

Prepared by the
East Midlands Economic Planning Council

Design by the Central Office of Information

The maps and illustrations in this Report have
been prepared by the East Midlands Regional
Office of the Ministry of Housing and Local
Government

ii

SBN 11 700415 4

Contents

LIST OF ILLUSTRATIONS

Plate

APPENDICES

Map inside back cover : East Midlands Region key map

ACKNOWLEDGEMENTS

Acknowledgement is made for photographs to Alfreton Urban District Council (Plate 8); Bentley Engineering Group Ltd.(Plate 2); The British United Shoe Machinery Co. Ltd. (Plate 5); Corby Development Corporation (Plate 6); Dunlop Polymer Engineering Division, Leicester (Plate 3); Northamptonshire Newspapers Ltd. (Plate 1); Rolls Royce Ltd (Plate 4); H. Tempest Industrial Ltd. IBP (Plate 7)

Foreword

This is the second report on the East Midlands to be published by the East Midlands Economic Planning Council. The first, *The East Midlands Study* published in December 1966, concluded with the words 'emphatically it is a Region where the opportunities outweigh the problems.' The first report was introduced by my friend, and predecessor as Chairman of the East Midlands Economic Planning Council, the late Mr. George Dearing, CBE. He contributed largely to the progress made during the first three years of the Council, and I can only hope that we have continued to develop along the path he marked out. We hope in this second examination - while not neglecting the problems - to examine the opportunities more fully and to describe what is being done and what needs to be done to make best use of them. The publication of the East Midlands Study was followed by a series of conferences and a multitude of other discussions, which have strengthened the confidence of the Council in its main conclusions, and lead on to the further proposals recorded in the present document.

Our object has been to determine the right pattern of development, which will enable the Region both to contribute most to the solution of national problems and the well-being of the national economy, and to provide opportunity and good environment for the people of the Region itself. Our conclusions will need re-examination in the light of the many reports on national economic and administrative problems, e.g. the Hunt Committee and the Royal Commission on Local Government expected during 1969. But even in advance of these reports, it seems to us desirable to restate the potentialities of the East Midlands. The Region is astride major communications linking the capital with the north, and the variety and strength of its economy must render its contribution and its point of view significant to national strategies.

Sir Mark Henig
Chairman, East Midlands Economic
Planning Council

EAST MIDLANDS ECONOMIC PLANNING COUNCIL

CHAIRMAN OF THE COUNCIL

Sir Mark Henig

Director, Henig & Sons Ltd., Leicester
Member, Leicester County Borough Council
Chairman, East Midlands Gas Consultative Council

MEMBERS

C. Adolphe

Midlands Divisional Officer, Union of Shop,
    Distributive and Allied Workers
Member, East Midlands Gas Consultative Council

Miss A. B. Allen

Chairman and Managing Director, Simon May & Co. Ltd

Alderman J. Anderson, CBE, JP

Locomotive driver
Member, Derbyshire County Council

Alderman K. W. Bowder, OBE

Solicitor
Member, Leicester County Borough Council

Alderman R. W. Chadburn, JP

Chairman, Mansfield Brewery Co. Ltd
Farmer
Member, Kesteven County Council

J. F. Coe

Transport and Distribution Manager,
    Stanton & Staveley Ltd (British Steel Corporation)

I. Drummond

Clerk and Solicitor of the Trent River Authority

A. C. Dugard, CBE

Chairman and Joint Managing Director,
    Cooper & Roe Ltd

Professor K. C. Edwards

Professor of Geography, University of Nottingham

C. T. Forsyth, CBE, JP

Management Consultant
Lately Managing Secretary, Nottingham Co-operative
    Society Ltd

Alderman E. S. Foster

Trade Development Officer, Nottingham Co-operative
    Society
Member, Nottingham County Borough Council

Professor S. J. Gould

Professor of Sociology, University of Nottingham

Alderman S. P. King, OBE, JP

District Organiser, National Union of Agricultural
    Workers
Member, Kesteven County Council
Chairman, Sheffield Regional Hospital Board

Councillor A. E. Lester, JP — Managing Director, Lesters (Nottm.) Ltd
Member, Nottinghamshire County Council

Col. P. H. Lloyd, CBE, TD, JP — Farmer
Chairman, Breedon & Cloud Hill Lime Works Ltd
and British Tar Products Ltd
Director, Martin's Bank (Birmingham District)
Chairman, Leicestershire County Council

Professor R. L. Meek — Tyler Professor of Economics, University of Leicester

H. L. Milliard, OBE, TD, JP — Secretary, Leicester and County Chamber of Commerce

W. L. Miron, OBE, TD, JP — Solicitor
Regional Chairman, National Coal Board

Alderman Mrs. D. P. Oxenham, JP — Vice-Chairman, Northamptonshire County Council
Deputy Chairman, Corby Development Corporation

H. E. Parkin — Area Secretary (Derbyshire), National Union of
Mineworkers

H. Pearson — Company Adviser on Engineering Methods,
Rolls Royce Ltd

H. C. Ryan — Chairman, Aveling-Barford Ltd
Director, The Leyland Motor Corporation Ltd

C. A. Unwin, JP — District Secretary (Midland and East Coast District),
General and Municipal Workers' Union

G. B. Walden, JP — District Organiser, Transport and General Workers'
Union, Northampton

K. J. Wilkinson — Chairman and Managing Director,
Spiral Tube (Heat Transfer) Ltd

CHAIRMAN, ECONOMIC PLANNING BOARD

J. W. Farnsworth

SECRETARY, ECONOMIC PLANNING COUNCIL

K. J. Price

Department of Economic Affairs,
Cranbrook House,
Cranbrook Street,
NOTTINGHAM.

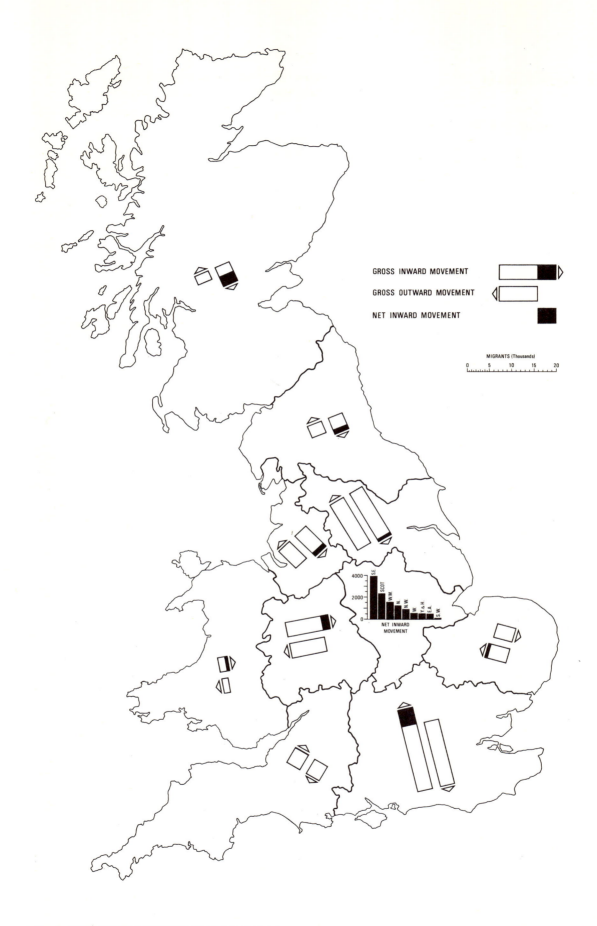

Fig. 1. MIGRATION BETWEEN EAST MIDLANDS AND OTHER ECONOMIC PLANNING REGIONS, SCOTLAND AND WALES, 1965-66

The information derives from the 1966 Census, 10% sample, and refers to movement in only one year 1965-66. See Appendix 1.

CHAPTER 1

The pattern of development

1.   The East Midlands is a region of opportunity. Confidence in its future is founded on its generally diversified economic activity, both in industry and agriculture, its past and present level of employment, and the relative absence of the disadvantages associated with massive and congested conurbations. More specifically, the following factors inspire such confidence :

(a)   The strategic position of the East Midlands within the heartland of the national economy, central to the great arc of industrial concentrations to the north, north-west, west and south.
(b)   The communication system, based on four national arteries, the M1 and A1 roads, and the East Coast and Midland railway routes.
(c)   The presence in strength in the industrial structure of the engineering and electrical industries, key growth industries in the nation at large.
(d)   The fact that the main industrial centres, while individually below conurbation scale, are sufficiently closely knit to provide some of the economic advantages of industrial concentration, including the size, mobility and diverse expertise of the labour-force, sub-contracting facilities, material and product movement, and social and educational services.
(e)   A growing population which will add stimulus to all existing industry; space for consequent development can be found without prejudice to the accepted principles of physical planning.

2.   We consider therefore that, despite the existence of immediate economic problems such as those of the Erewash Valley, and the likelihood that others will emerge with changes in basic technology, the position, history and structure of the Region are such that it should be possible to resolve the problems of maintaining viability and increasing prosperity.

3.   It is clear that the key problem is that of population. The United Kingdom can expect a considerable increase in population during the rest of the century; it is faced with the problem not only of housing this increased population but of ensuring that it is employed in ways which produce a rising standard of life in surroundings of increasing amenity. Technological progress in the United Kingdom is such that these problems can be met with confidence.

4.   So much of the population increase will take place in the large, essentially unplanned conurbations Britain has inherited that there can be little doubt that existing policies to move some industry and some population out of those conurbations into new or expanded towns must continue. This problem of a congested conurbation does not arise — at least as yet — in the East Midlands, but the Region does include some of the areas of planned expansion, and should be prepared to agree to others if this is nationally desirable. The creation of entirely new communities, or the deliberate planned expansion of small existing ones, does not, however, represent the only outcome of the rise in population. So long as there are attractive jobs to be found people are likely to move to fill them; public authority will still have to plan environment, but the moves themselves may be a purely private concern. We expect that the population of the Region will be increased in this way too. Movement into the Region during 1965/66 is shown in Fig.1 (page viii) and Appendix 1. It will be seen that there was in that year a net inward balance of migration from every other region in the country. But the most important factor is likely to be the natural increase of the population already here.

5.   The Council has studied the existing population figures and the most reliable projections for the future, the industrial structure of the Region and such changes in it as can reasonably be foreseen and the physical environment, both natural and man-made. It has also taken into account the social context in which all these elements are embodied and has reached the following conclusions:

(a)   That a rising standard of living with increasing amenity should be readily attainable for the population of the East Midlands.
(b)   That the Region is likely to continue to offer opportunities of employment and environmental advantages in a manner which will encourage a balance of voluntary migration to it.
(c)   That if it should be desirable in the national interest to add to the number of new or expanded towns, this will be possible without bringing into question the foregoing conclusions.

6.   We referred in the East Midlands Study to the industrial zone of Nottinghamshire/Derbyshire as an incipient conurbation. We do not regard this as a danger to be avoided, but as a warning that good planning will be required to accommodate an increasing population without creating the congestion and poor environment characteristic of the older conurbations.

7.   The East Midlands Study was criticised in some quarters for accepting too readily that a considerable rise in the Region's population was not to be resisted. Whatever the general problems arising from population growth may be, we are of the opinion that, so far as this Region is concerned, a further increase would in many respects be beneficial. The short answer, however, is that an increase in population is to be expected, and that it would be unwise not to prepare for it.

8.   Planning in the East Midlands must be concerned with creating the conditions which will foster economic growth and a rise in productivity and real income per head. This implies the identification of some places as suitable for growth, and of others which have not this promise.

9.   Neither the scale of population increase as predicted for the Region during the next few decades nor the likely programme of industrial development would appear to justify the creation of new towns on virgin sites. On the other hand many existing centres in the Region are capable of expansion; many indeed would, as communities, profit from growth and the problem therefore is largely one of identifying those centres which already exhibit growth tendencies or in which, for sound economic and social reasons, growth should be encouraged.

10.   The physical development of particular localities must be guided by local studies, and we are happy to note that these are proceeding. The main developments are:

(a)   A joint study of the Nottinghamshire/Derbyshire area (excluding only the Peak Park Area) undertaken by a Unit established by the four local planning authorities of Derby, Derbyshire, Nottingham and Nottinghamshire. The need for this study was stressed in our first publication and it is gratifying that the Unit is now at work.
(b)   A joint study of Leicester and Leicestershire undertaken by a Unit established by the two local planning authorities who were due to receive its report by the end of 1968.
(c)   An interdepartmental study of the area of Northampton, south Northamptonshire, Bedford and Buckinghamshire, which has been accepted as suitable for large-scale expansion to take population and industry from the London area. This general project crosses regional boundaries, but it is right that the whole area should be studied as a unit. Its findings will have significance to a much wider area than that of the study itself, and it will be necessary to evaluate them, as regards the East Midlands in respect of Northamptonshire generally.
(d)   The local planning authorities of Kesteven, Holland and Rutland are collecting information for a sub-regional study.

THE SCALE OF ECONOMIC DEVELOPMENT

11. The main components of the national economy are the great industrial concentrations including the major ports. Some of these are massive, Birmingham and the Black Country for instance rivalling the Ruhr in industrial intensity, and there are few other comparable concentrations in Europe. The industrial region in fact is the characteristic feature of the spatial pattern to which the economy of modern Britain has given rise.

12. The first need of every business is to maintain its competitive position. In manufacturing industry various factors concerned in meeting this need generally result in a geographical concentration of activity. Such factors include access to supplies (including materials and power); to sub-contractors, who are each likely to be working for a number of producers; to labour, skilled and unskilled, male and female; and to markets, as well as opportunities for specialisation as between firms in an industrial area.

13. Present-day conditions, however, contain elements which may favour greater dispersal of industrial activity. Thus the trend away from labour-intensive production towards capital-intensive production reduces the significance of labour supply as a locational factor. Other technological advances may also promote greater flexibility. Changes in the source of power provide an example, in that electricity and gas today exert less influence upon location than water-power and coal once did. Similarly, up-to-date methods of communication in management control (telephones, computers, etc.) reduce the necessity for concentration. Again, improvements in transport for the movement of goods and people are likely to promote new patterns of industrial distribution which can attain the same density of supply and demand as that achieved by traditional factors in the older concentrations. Among other factors favouring dispersal are the economic disadvantages of urban congestion which are especially manifest in the existing conurbations. These include the prevalence of old and inefficient factory buildings, high rents, bottlenecks in the transport system and, for many employees, undesirably long journeys to work. The higher standards now demanded in both living and working conditions can often be more readily and more cheaply satisfied in less congested areas.

14. Doubtless the existing concentrations offer many locational advantages and the diversity of activity in broadly-based industrial areas helps to sustain full employment in periods of industrial recession or technological change. When more factory space is required by a firm, ease of management control and economy in the use of common services usually make an extension of existing premises or development on a nearby site advantageous. On the other hand the need for heavy additional investment in plant and buildings may justify development further away in order to avoid the shortage of land, and possibly labour, near the original site.

Nottinghamshire/Derbyshire sub-region

15. If this sub-region, with its population of 1,764,000 in 1967 expected to increase to 1,982,000 by 1981, is considered in the light of these arguments, it becomes apparent that growth areas must be identified which will offer an appropriate balance between concentration and dispersal to meet various industrial needs. The most flexible way to achieve this is to guide future development towards centres of high potentiality which lie at some distance from the large, vigorous and more fully established centres. In time such places would progress from a supplementary to a complementary role. Both Nottingham and Derby are vigorous and well established centres and in this sub-region the area of potentiality clearly lies to the north and could well be located along the line joining Alfreton, Sutton and Mansfield.

16. Still further north the Chesterfield-Staveley and Worksop areas which were originally dependent on the Sheffield area, in terms of economic function, show distinct possibilities of becoming complementary to it - and the process is marked already in the case of Chesterfield.

3

17.   Nottingham and Derby, together with Leicester, form the urban centre of the Region but whereas Leicester is located at a distance from the others and in that sense is a free-standing city, the other two lie close together, their centres being only 15 miles apart, and their fringes linked by intervening areas of urban development. Much of the intervening built-up area, including the town of Long Eaton, parts of Beeston and Stapleford and the adjoining district of Sandiacre, comprises amorphous development of which the individual parts are distinguishable only in terms of local authority boundaries. Greater Nottingham is in fact rapidly becoming a vast urban tract which, with Derby and the lower Erewash Valley, is in danger of becoming a continuous area of urban development exhibiting the characteristics of a traditional conurbation. The problem is one of guiding future development without inhibiting the natural growth of the two leading centres. Planning techniques should be adequate to ensure that this growth is acceptably shaped. The results of the Nottinghamshire/Derbyshire study mentioned in para. 10(a) will be particularly relevant in this context.

18.   Clearly an unplanned sprawl must be avoided but modern transport makes it possible to provide the advantages of large economic scale with the degree of dispersal which physical factors require. It would be better to regard Nottingham, Derby and the upper Erewash as focal points within a single cluster of towns than to consider each of them as separate entities. The significant economic unit is no longer the separate town or even the medium-sized city.

19.   There is already considerable daily movement and economic inter-dependence within the area, and a maintenance of existing policies of restriction of industrial development and urban sprawl at Nottingham and Derby with relaxation in the southern parts of the Nottinghamshire/Derbyshire coalfield would create a better industrial and population balance, without detriment to the natural economic growth of the two major centres. It would indeed limit the attraction to them of population from near-by areas presently suffering from employment problems. A similar problem arises in the relationship between the northern part of this area and Sheffield.

20.   The Nottinghamshire/Derbyshire coalfield forms the largest single industrial area within the Region. A line drawn through Nottingham and Mansfield broadly divides it into two sections, a western portion, largely though not wholly in Derbyshire, in which coalmining, iron working and other forms of industrial activity developed earlier, and an eastern portion, lying in west Nottinghamshire, in which industrial development took place later and less intensively. The western portion, drained by the Erewash to the south and the Rother to the north, is densely populated. It comprises a relatively narrow but concentrated industrial belt stretching for some 40 miles from the Trent near Long Eaton to the outskirts of Sheffield. With the successive closure of iron-making plants, the concentration of foundries, and the continuing decline in coalmining, at an accelerating rate in recent years, the traditional basis of the economy has become seriously threatened. Positive measures are therefore required to replace the local employment opportunities lost in the older trades to ensure a balanced employment structure for the future. This is essential if the area is to avoid a progressive decline in population. The area is in some places further handicapped by the legacy of its earlier industrial phase — colliery spoil heaps, disused railway tracks, dilapidated and obsolescent property, ground affected by mining subsidence; but these are far from universal and are remediable. Moreover many of the existing settlements are scattered, shapeless, and often rather deficient in amenities and services. On the other hand the area has distinct advantages. In terms of industrial development, it lies between the large centres of Sheffield, Nottingham and Derby; it has available industrial sites and a steady supply of versatile manpower; it is served by a major railway route, the line from London (St. Pancras) to Leeds and the north, while the passage of the London-Yorkshire motorway (M1) through the area provides an added location advantage. What is needed, in addition to new sources of employment, is a systematic renovation of the physical environment together with a planned re-grouping of the settlements which will provide the setting for a new era of economic activity. Urban planning should aim at a new relationship among many small existing settlements.

4

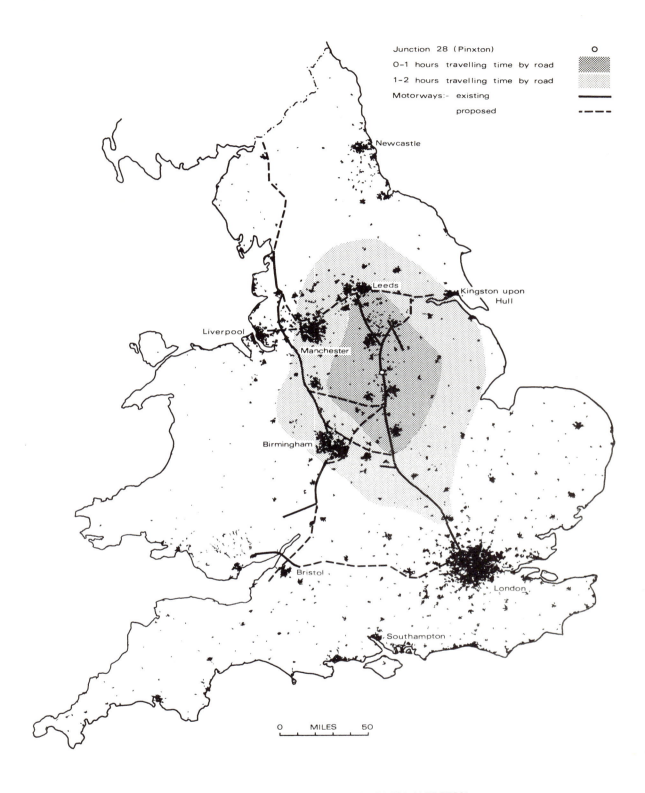

Junction 28 (Pinxton)   O

0-1 hours travelling time by road

1-2 hours travelling time by road

Motorways:- existing

proposed

Newcastle

Leeds

Kingston upon Hull

Liverpool

Manchester

Birmingham

Bristol

London

Southampton

0   MILES   50

Fig. 2. AREAS WITHIN 1 HOUR AND 2 HOUR TRAVEL DISTANCE FROM ALFRETON

The areas are within 1 hour and 2 hour travel by vehicle from the M.1 access point nearest Alfreton,
at average speeds of 55 m.p.h. on the motorway and 35 m.p.h. on other main roads.

The Leicester sub-region

21.   In the Leicestershire and south Derbyshire coalfield a repetition of the environmental disadvantages of the major coalfield occurs. The Derbyshire portion is worse than its Leicestershire counterpart in this respect, due to the industrial dereliction and disturbance of the ground caused by the clay-working and pipeworks in the Swadlincote district. Both areas share the same prospect of a decline in coalmining although the pipe-making industry shows no immediate sign of waning. Alternative sources of employment might well be found in Burton on Trent or even in Derby itself, but a programme of environmental improvement similar to that advocated for the main Nottinghamshire and Derbyshire coalfield will be necessary for the Swadlincote district if it is to remain acceptable for residence and local employment. In the Leicestershire portion of the coalfield, development originating in Leicester may well be sufficient to provide alternative sources of employment for those affected by colliery closures in the Coalville district. If some re-grouping of population over the coalfield as a whole becomes necessary, consideration should be given to the old market-town of Ashby-de-la-Zouch as a focus. Ashby lies between the two active portions of the coalfield and between Derby and Leicester. It is on the trunk road (eventually to be greatly improved) between Nottingham and Birmingham and is only a few miles from the M1 motorway. It is situated in pleasant country free from the scars of industry, while its position gives it potentiality for an expansion of population and services.

22.   The solutions depend on the future envisaged for the whole area centring on Burton on Trent and Lichfield; if at any stage this area is to be expanded in industrial and population terms, social investment in Swadlincote could well be worthwhile. At the appropriate time a study involving parts of Derbyshire, Leicestershire and Staffordshire would seem desirable; it might well follow the completion of the Leicester/Leicestershire Study.

23.   A similar need for inter-regional study arises in the case of Hinckley and the smaller Leicestershire communities associated with it. The links with Nuneaton, Coventry and the West Midlands are hardly less than with Leicester, and further study of the development of this area must at some stage involve joint action across the county and regional boundaries. Both the problems arising from over-dependence on one industry and the potentialities implicit in location justify this further attention.

24.   The population of the sub-region is expected to rise by 1981 to 791,000 from its 1967 level of 695,000, much of which is concentrated in and near Leicester which, because of its separate physical identity, presents so far as expansion is concerned less of a problem than those parts of the sub-region already mentioned. There are areas within the existing city boundary in which growth can be accommodated and there are neighbouring small centres suitable for dormitory and satellite development.

25.   There can be little doubt that but for the restraints imposed by government policy on the location of industry, Leicester would grow rapidly in terms of population and industry. Even despite this policy the economic advantages of the area are so great that further growth seems inevitable. In the East Midlands Study we took the view that the process of gradual accretion to the city all round its perimeter would produce difficult problems, and that it would be desirable to encourage development in specific directions as an alternative. The precise physical pattern must be left to the local authority study to which reference has been made; it must be compatible with the great vigour of the local economy.

26.   The industrial and technological basis of Loughborough is also of significance for future development, and needs to be considered in relation to any conclusions about Leicester itself. Social and industrial ties with Leicester are already close.

Northamptonshire sub-region

27.   Recent proposals for development in Northamptonshire and in places not far beyond its boundary bring a new significance to the southern extremity of the East Midlands Region and the adjoining parts of the East Anglia and South East Regions. The area lies only 50-60 miles from London and, being served by the A1 and M1 and by rapid railway services, it is in many respects especially suitable for the accommodation of overspill population and to relieve the congestion of industry in the capital. Town development schemes at Wellingborough and Daventry (already in progress), at Northampton and Peterborough and the project for a New Town at Milton Keynes in Buckinghamshire will all require the creation of new sources of employment or the expansion of existing ones. It is important that this should be fully realised in view of the possible contraction of the footwear industry in mid-Northamptonshire and of the special problem affecting the New Town of Corby, which already has a population of 47,000 and needs further industry. Further development of the steel industry at Corby is unlikely to demand an increase in the existing and predominantly male labour force. The need for employment for women remains, as it has done for years past, an essential requirement for the well-being of this community. It has a predominantly young population and a higher than average birth rate, so economic safeguards for the future must be sought. The situation is further complicated by the changing relations between Corby and the nearby town of Kettering (39,000)*, for the former now exceeds the latter in size, whereas not long ago the reverse was decidedly the case. Notwithstanding the change, Corby is economically less balanced and has a less representative age-distribution than Kettering. Since at any time the amount of industry able to move is limited it would certainly be wrong to neglect the interests of Corby while encouraging growth elsewhere in the county at its expense.

28.   The planned growth in these areas and the age distribution which results help to account for the rapid increase in population: this is expected to raise the 1967 total of 434,000 to 640,000 by 1981. Assuming that population and industry can develop together in time as well as in place, there remains the problem of organising a satisfactory spatial structure for the resultant urban expansion and this requires the careful co-ordination of plans promoted by the relevant local authorities.

29.   The importance of Northampton as the sub-regional centre for the towns of mid-Northamptonshire must not be obscured by present plans to build up to a town with at least 200,000 inhabitants as part of associated development involving Bedfordshire and Buckinghamshire as well. Further east, the development of Peterborough will have significance for the Region. The growth of Peterborough (outside the regional boundary) should be planned to take account of related residential expansion in the adjoining counties; it is important to preserve the character of the neighbouring parts of Northamptonshire. The developments of Northampton and Peterborough, taken together, will in the longer term have a profound effect on the economy and structure of neighbouring areas.

The Eastern Lowlands

30.   The economy of the Eastern Lowlands has been based on a very prosperous agriculture but here as elsewhere the demand for agricultural manpower is declining; the influence of Peterborough, Nottingham and Lincoln itself will provide some of the economic bases needed to compensate for this. In the east, however, there is no town of comparable size, and it is there that the problem is most likely to be acute.

31.   The population of the sub-region is nevertheless expected to increase from 402,000 in 1967 to 447,000 in 1981. The largest community is the City of Lincoln which has shown considerable capacity for growth. It will moreover be in a strategic position in relation to the further expansion of south Humberside, and the pace rather than the fact of the further economic development of Lincoln is likely to depend on decisions taken about the Humber area.

---

8   * Source: G.R.O. 1967 estimates.

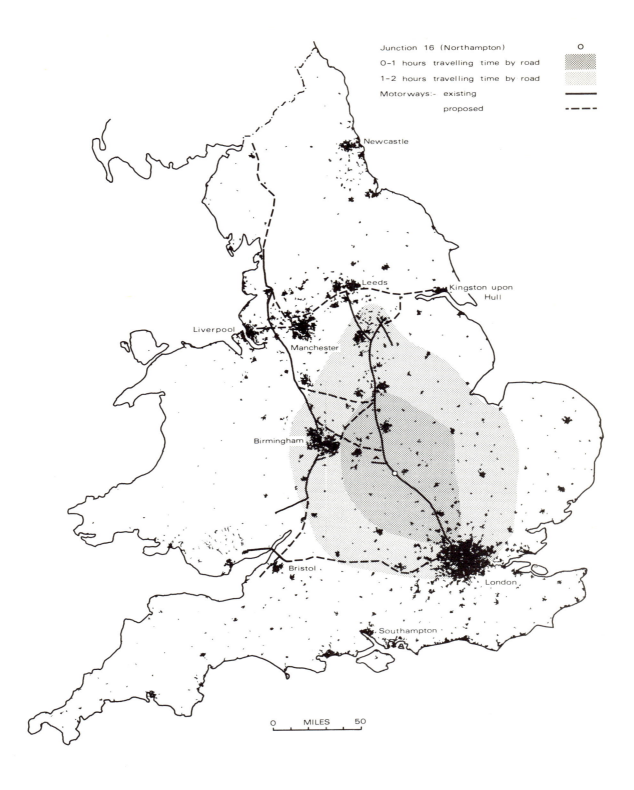

Junction 16 (Northampton) ⊙

0–1 hours travelling time by road

1–2 hours travelling time by road

Motorways:- existing

proposed

Newcastle

Leeds

Kingston upon Hull

Liverpool

Manchester

Birmingham

Bristol

London

Southampton

0 MILES 50

Fig. 3. AREAS WITHIN 1 HOUR AND 2 HOUR TRAVEL DISTANCE FROM NORTHAMPTON

The areas are within 1 hour and 2 hour travel by vehicle from the M.1 access point nearest Northampton, at average speeds of 55 m.p.h. on the motorway and 35 m.p.h. on other main roads.

32.   Grantham (26,000)*, along with Newark (25,000)* and Retford (19,000)* in Nottinghamshire, is situated on the main railway from London (King's Cross) to the north and alongside the Great North Road, and is capable of further industrial expansion and population growth. Clearly, a wider range of employment opportunities, including greater scope for female employment, would benefit all these towns but with the existing substantial commitments for the transfer of industry and population from London to Northamptonshire and such places as Bedford and Peterborough and the proposed New Town at Milton Keynes, it is unlikely that major growth will be possible in the next ten years.

33.   The growth of Lincoln and Peterborough, together with any of the developments foreshadowed in the previous paragraphs, will affect all the neighbouring communities. There is indeed considerable daily movement already from country areas into the large towns, and the need for some local industry in these communities to give employment to members of commuters' families is increasingly apparent. Both these cities are separated from part of their natural hinterland by an inter-regional boundary and close co-operation between authorities on both sides is needed.

34.   Outside the range of Lincoln and Peterborough there are even more difficult problems in east Lincolnshire, where the traditional pattern of market towns has been undermined by reductions in agricultural manpower. There is therefore a need to encourage some limited but significant development of Boston as a focal point in this area. Its advantages as a port are not of cardinal importance, so attention to its land communications is of great significance to the whole of Holland and southern Lindsey.

The small towns of particular character

35.   Some of the smaller towns of the Region, because of their distinctive character in terms of historical interest or architectural merit, should not be encouraged to expand by the introduction of large-scale industrial growth. They should be maintained more or less at their present size, with any future increase resulting from mainly natural growth. Among the larger of these the following may be cited: Ashbourne (6,000)*; Bakewell (4,000)*, the administrative centre of the Peak National Park; Melbourne (4,000)ᵩ, with its fine Norman church and adjacent Hall and grounds, the centre of a rich district of intensive cultivation; Southwell (4,000)ᵩ, which has been in some danger of losing its character by excessive development as a dormitory centre for Nottingham; Stamford (13,000)*, a town distinguished by its unusually high proportion of buildings in the local stone of outstanding architectural merit. Many smaller centres, of which Rockingham may suffice as an example, give character and charm to their areas and collectively to the Region as a whole. Conservation must indeed be accompanied by adaptation, and some growth may be welcomed, so long as it maintains rather than destroys the essential character of these towns.

PHYSICAL PATTERN OF REGIONAL DEVELOPMENT

36.   Looking at the whole Region we see the most desirable pattern of development as being:

(a)   The development of industry on the Alfreton-Sutton-Mansfield line to act as a magnet for some of the growth arising in the Nottingham/Derby area, with adequate investment in infrastructure and adequate governmental steering and support of industry to make it viable.

(b)   Continued development in the Chesterfield and Worksop areas, on the same basis in relation to Sheffield, as in *(a)*.

(c)   An acceptance that in the south a new industrial concentration is to be created, with Northampton as a primary focus, but with sufficient attention to the contribution of the other industrial towns of Northamptonshire.

---

* Source: G.R.O. 1967 estimates..
ᵩ Source: 1961 Census.

(d) The preservation, or restoration, of open spaces and good environment around and within each of these areas of industrial concentration to preserve the amenity and social identity of their component towns. This is of particular significance in relation to the middle Trent Valley where pressures on land use have been most acute.

(e) The continued expansion of Leicester as a free-standing town and of Loughborough as an area of technological importance.

(f) A further study of the Leicestershire and south Derbyshire coalfield in its relation to parts of Staffordshire.

(g) A readiness to encourage small developments in Newark, Grantham and possibly other Lincolnshire towns as a base for further expansion at a later date. Greater immediate importance is attached to a limited but significant measure of development at Boston to provide for better employment opportunities in the area. To this it must be added that expansion in Lincoln itself, and perhaps elsewhere, may be greatly accelerated if positive decisions are made about Humberside.

CHAPTER 2

Population

37.   Revised estimates show a likelihood that the regional increase in population will be a little smaller or slower than was suggested in the East Midlands Study. Instead of an increase in population of 730,000 by 1981, we now expect only some 565,000, a difference of 165,000. Of this difference, a large part (nearly 90,000) is the adjustment to take into account the extension of Sheffield across the former boundaries of the Region - not only has the present population figure needed to be deducted but the original projections included a planned overspill from Sheffield and its natural increase which is now excluded. But in fact the objective situation is unaltered by the boundary change; the people will live and work just where they would have done in any event. This is, however, the only substantial alteration made to the estimates of movement in and out of the Region. So far as can be estimated, the scale of planned movement into Northamptonshire and of private migration into the Region suggested in the Study remain about right. The balance of the difference is due to a reduction in the expected birth rate and, of course, to the elapse of two years since the last report, which means we are now concerned with only fourteen years. The new figures are given in the table below.

Table 1   Home Population (thousands) *

	1967	1971	1981
All ages	3,295	3,434	3,860
Children 0-14	782	855	1,013
Men 15-64	1,077	1,093	1,204
Women 15-59	954	969	1,078
Working Age 15-59/64	2,031	2,062	2,282
Elderly 60/65+	482	517	567

* As each figure has been rounded to the nearest whole the totals are not necessarily the sum of their components.

38.   The change in the anticipated number of births in the period up to 1981 will, of course, affect only the numbers under the age of 15. The total in that year is expected to be 1,013,000 instead of 1,085,000. This might have marginally relieved some of the expected pressure on the education system and would have slowed the deterioration in the ratio of the economically active to those dependent on them. However, planned raising of the school-leaving age in 1972-3 will raise the number of children under this age to 1,078,000 in 1981. Some of the 15-year-olds would undoubtedly have been staying at school without the compulsory raising of the leaving age - 17.8% were doing so in 1964 and the proportion was rising - but on the other hand an increasing proportion of those over 16 can be expected to be staying at school voluntarily or undertaking other full-time further education.

39.   For the next few years the increase in the number of people in the working age group is likely to be much less than the increases in the numbers either under school-leaving age or over

normal working ages. This will be made more obvious by the raising of the school-leaving age; even fewer will enter the working age group. In consequence, by mid-1973 the number of people of working age will probably be about the same as in 1967. Even this takes into account a steady movement of workers into the Region. But with this continued movement, and the effect of the rise in births round 1960, this situation will ease later in the decade. By 1981 the number of men and women of working age is expected to rise by 184,000 over the 1967 figure even after allowing for raising of the school-leaving age. This compares with a total increase, for all age groups, of 565,000, and the proportion of people who are of working age will have fallen. Apart from the effects of the boundary change, the numbers in the age group 60+ (women)/65+ (men) are unchanged from the Study figures. The details are given in paragraph 41 and Table 2 below.

40.   The planned movements into Northamptonshire will be responsible for a considerable proportion of the increase in the working age group, particularly the younger section. In those areas unaffected by planned migration - Derby, Leicester and Nottingham - the population of working age will increase much more slowly proportionately; it is likely that the Eastern Lowlands sub-region will have the slowest increase and that in the Leicester sub-region there will be a slight fall in population of working age by 1971. Unless adequate alternative opportunities are provided, the loss of job opportunities due to pit closures is likely largely to exclude the particular areas affected from attracting net private migration, which will tend to be concentrated in areas where opportunities are greater.

Table 2   Home Population Changes (thousands)*

	1967-71		1971-81		1967-81	
	No.	%	No.	%	No.	%
All ages	139	4.2	426	12.4	565	17.1
Children 0-14	73	9.3	158	18.5	231	31.2
Men 15-64	16	1.5	110	10.1	126	11.8
Women 15-59	15	1.6	108	11.1	123	11.9
Working Age 15-59/64	31	1.5	218	10.6	249	11.9
Elderly 60/65+	35	7.1	50	9.7	85	17.6

* As each figure has been rounded to the nearest whole the totals are not necessarily the sum of their components.

41.   Throughout the 1970s the proportion of the population in the working age group will continue to decline (from 616 per thousand in 1967 to 600 in 1971 and 591 in 1981 or 574 when adjusted for the increase in school-leaving age). The 1981 figure in the East Midlands Study was 584, the present estimate of 591 reflecting the effect of the fall in the expected birth-rate on the number of young dependants. Sub-regionally Leicester and then Nottinghamshire/Derbyshire are expected to suffer the greatest proportionate reductions. Despite the effects of migration after 1971 the Northampton Sub-Region is expected to show a fall up to 1981 after allowance for raising the school-leaving age in 1972-3.

42.   The net effect of these changes is that the population of working age in the Region is expected to increase by nearly 12% (of whom an increasing proportion will be engaged in full-time education) but will have to support an increase in the total population of more than 17%. This implies the need for a much greater output per head if the improvement in the standard of living is to be maintained. This can be achieved by greater productivity through mechanisation and improved work methods; also, perhaps, to some extent by drawing on labour reserves.

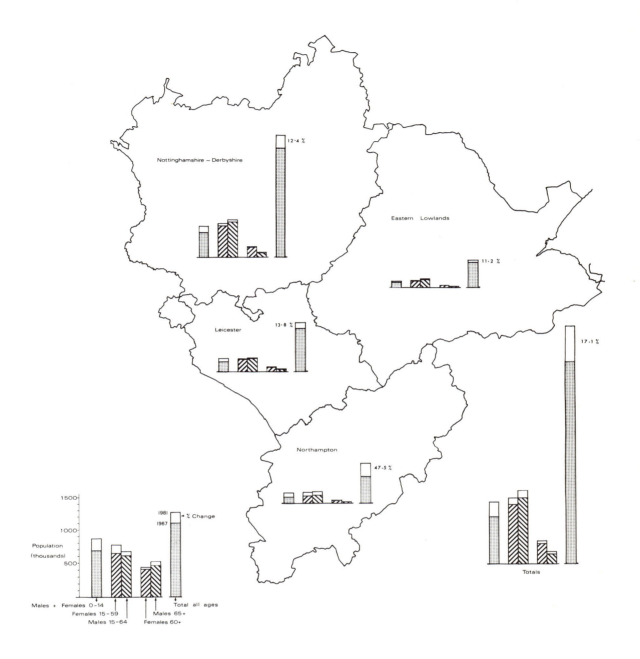

Fig. 4. POPULATION CHANGES 1967-81

See Appendix 4.

Table 3   Population of working age per thousand persons, all ages

	1967	1971	1981
East Midlands	616	600	591 (574)*
Nottinghamshire/Derbyshire	621	606	593 (576)
Leicester	615	593	578 (561)
Eastern Lowlands	615	603	602 (583)
Northamptonshire	601	588	591 (577)

* The figures in brackets are the 1981 proportions adjusted for the expected raising of the school-leaving age in 1972-3.

43.   In the East Midlands, the labour reserve of men of working age is small and any significant contribution could only come from a higher activity rate in the elderly age group. The reserve of unoccupied women may be an important source of additional labour, although experience since 1951 has been that the increase in the number of occupied women has been almost entirely of those in part-time employment. This is likely to continue to be the case and industry will note the organisational implications.

CHAPTER 3

The economy of the East Midlands

44.   The main reasons for confidence in the future of the East Midlands were outlined in Chapter 1, but the economic basis is so fundamental to all plans for the future that something more needs to be said.

45.   Despite the importance of mining and agriculture to the economy of the Region, the most characteristic activity is manufacture. The significant feature is that the industrial structure is highly diverse (in this it approximates to the national position) and this diversity is widely spread among industrial centres which are in general well linked with each other. Inevitably there are aspects of the region's economy - as in that of any community - that are weaker than others. Some of the industries with high net output per head are not represented in great strength, and several of the traditional industries that are strongly represented have been - though the situation is changing - labour intensive rather than capital intensive. In consequence income per head was found in the East Midlands Study to be rather below the national average. None the less, the Study recognised a general condition of prosperity, one consequence of which has been that the Region as a whole has suffered from manpower shortages. This condition is likely to continue and could remain an important factor inhibiting the economic growth of the Region; but it will be offset by increasing mechanisation and reduced demand for labour in declining industries. The likely balance in the near future is discussed in paragraphs 53 to 55 below.

46.   Statements such as the foregoing and the importance which may be attached to the low unemployment rates which the Region experienced over a long period of years inevitably attract criticism when made at a time of general economic difficulty and of increase in unemployment. Certainly the Region has not escaped, and cannot escape, the consequences of restraints on the national economy. The economic advantages of the East Midlands are relative to the national context; when the economy is slack the Region will suffer less than many others and when activity increases it will more rapidly reach the point where manpower shortage becomes a restraining factor.

47.   It is against this background that the analysis to be found in Chapter 6 of the East Midlands Study must be read. It may be sufficient here to quote the conclusion of paragraph 219 that

'On balance then, compared with Great Britain, the East Midlands had a slightly smaller proportion of employees in expanding industries and a far bigger one in contracting industries, but the expanding industries, as a whole, were growing more quickly and the contracting industries declining more slowly than throughout the country as a whole. The net result for all industries (including services) over the period 1959/63 was a regional growth of 6% against 4½% for Britain as a whole.'

48.   In the paragraph quoted the reference to 'expanding' and 'contracting' industries was to expansion or contraction in terms of the labour force, not of volume or value of output. This does, however, foreshadow real and continuing problems for the Region for a long time to come. The significant industries in the Region where contraction of employment may take place are those of

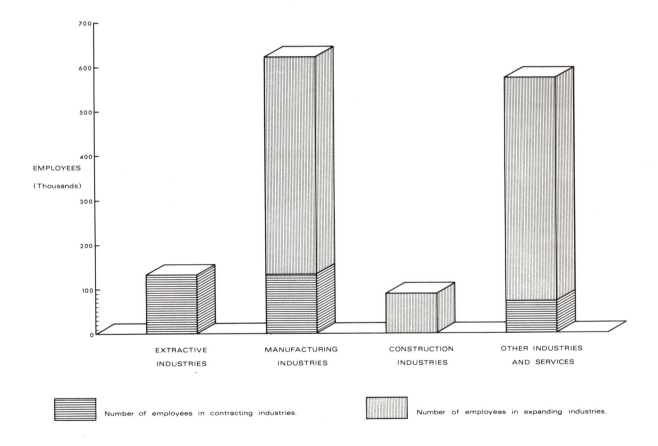

Fig. 5. EMPLOYMENT IN EXPANDING AND CONTRACTING INDUSTRIES, 1967

The volume of the columns represents the total number of employees in employment in four broad industrial groupings in 1967 and the shaded areas show the proportions in expanding and contracting industries based on growth rates observed in the Region 1961-66.

coalmining, footwear, hosiery and knitwear, and agriculture. In the case of agriculture the indications point to a continuing rise in output produced by a contracting labour force, but of all the others it can clearly be said that they can only retain and develop their markets if there is a continuous rise in productivity per head, and that it is extremely doubtful whether any such rise will be matched by an increase in demand sufficient to maintain an unaltered labour force. In the case of footwear and hosiery the factors of international competition, changes in method, and changes in fashion are strong; these factors almost inevitably lead to a succession of short-term difficulties and sometimes triumphs in terms of trade, but the short-term changes do not obscure the probability that a long-term rise in output per head will also mean a long-term fall in the total numbers employed.

49.   In an attempt to get a clearer picture of the future of hosiery and associated industry in the Region, a Study Group constituted of prominent individuals connected with the textile industry was set up under the auspices of the Ministry of Technology to consider the likely developments in the uses of textile fibres. A fuller account is given in Appendix 8, but the following points may be noted:

(a)   Man-made fibre production, mainly rayon and nylon, was carried on at only one location in the Region. Although the proportions of the different types might change, it seemed likely that fibres would continue to be produced in the Region for the foreseeable future. Not all of the fibres went into textiles and the large proportion used to make filter-tips for cigarettes was a stabilising factor. No plan to introduce any new types of fibre production to Spondon was known but the productivity of the plant was being steadily improved and this should ensure its continued profitability.

(b)   The knitting industry was the most important part of the textile industry in the Region. It had a bright future providing certain steps were taken. The knitting industry itself believed that with lower fibre prices it had nothing to fear. However, the age of the factory buildings and the fragmentation of the industry could prove to be serious handicaps and the industry had been criticised for employing far too few production engineers. Steps were being taken to overcome these deficiencies, but it was clear that a continuous policy of re-investment in buildings and plant would be necessary to meet the steadily increasing foreign competition.

(c)   If they were to take advantage of these developments, it was clear that the textile machinery manufacturers must also move ahead as rapidly as they could.

50.   The problem in coalmining is more acute than that in the other industries mentioned in paragraph 48. The transition from a two-fuel to a four-fuel economy has brought about a reduced demand for coal, and although there is controversy as to the extent and speed with which this reduction will continue, the seriousness of the position is undoubted. The chain of generating stations down the Trent Valley, some of the biggest of which are still under construction, is of great importance to the future of the coalmining industry and will maintain that importance for many years, because many of the collieries in the Region are amongst the most economic in the country, and are therefore in a strong position to meet competition from other fuels. Since the expenditure on these stations, which were designed to burn coal, has been firmly committed, the industry has at present an in-built advantage so far as power production in the Midlands is concerned. The advent of nuclear power and natural gas will affect this in the long term but in the meantime any prospect of limiting fall in demand depends on continuing to improve productivity per head and so keeping prices competitive with other fuels. In this context it is worth noting that there has not been an increase in the pithead price of industrial coal produced in the Region since September, 1960. Competitiveness will be helped by the continuation of the industry's programme of modernisation and concentration on the most efficient pits but the result must be that over the next fifteen years the number of men employed in the industry will be very substantially reduced. The future rate of run-down in this Region has been variously forecast and seems likely to average between 3,000 and 4,500 per year over the next few years. This is not very different from past rates of run-down, largely due to voluntary departure from the pits and age retirement. Provided that a substantial number of the under-55-year-old men are prepared to move to the pits which are

staying open, the redundancy problem, though serious to the individuals affected, should not be large in terms of total numbers and it could be that a greater difficulty for the industry may be the maintenance of an adequate labour force in the productive pits. The main aspect affecting long-term regional planning is, however, the replacement of the lost job opportunities.

51.   On the information at present available it is not possible to define precisely the extent of the East Midlands' contribution to the national economy in terms of increase of the national wealth.*
Nevertheless, by looking at the employment figures for the Region's manufacturing industries in comparison with those for Great Britain as a whole, some idea may be obtained of the scale of contribution.   In these terms the picture is reassuring; the number of employees in employment in the East Midlands approximates to 6.2% of the number in Great Britain but the numbers of people employed in manufacturing industry are 7.2 per cent of the national figure of those so employed. The significant manufacturing industries in terms of employment may be considered to be:

   (a)   metal manufacture;
   (b)   engineering and electrical goods;
   (c)   vehicles, aircraft, etc.; and
   (d)   other metal goods.

In groups (a), (b) and (c) the Region's employees are respectively 7.8%, 6.4% and 6.5% of those employed nationally in the same groups; in (d) they are considerably below the ratio of 6.2% of employees in employment. The growth rates of (a), (b) and (d) also compare very favourably with the national figures. The decline in (c) is due to the preponderance in this Region of aircraft engine manufacture, employment in which fell from a very high level in 1960 to a low in 1962. Since then it has been increasing steadily but has not yet recovered to the high figure of 1960. Another indication of the scale of the Region's contribution to the national economy derives from comparison of regional industrial investment. Although comprehensive figures are not available, the information from investment grant statistics is encouraging. Of the expenditure on plant and machinery for manufacturing and ship-repairing which received grants in the year ended 31st March, 1968 under the Industrial Development Act 1966, 8 per cent was in the East Midlands.

52.   Contraction in employment in certain manufacturing industries will pose two distinct questions: whether the expanding industries will be able to absorb the manpower thus released, and whether those industries, or units of them, will be located in the right places for this absorption to be feasible. The analysis of the manner in which expanding industries are represented in the Region, and particularly the diversity and wide spread of the engineering sectors, gives confidence that in any normal national economic conditions reductions in the manpower of footwear and textiles will be more than matched by other demands for labour. No doubt local and temporary difficulties will occur, as always in large-scale industrial changes, but the underlying position seems as strong as can reasonably be hoped for.

53.   An attempt has been made to assess the probable balance of labour demand and supply in 1975 by considering changes which have already taken place and by making allowance for known trends. Forecasts for such a period ahead are hazardous, involving, as they do, assumptions about activity and migration rates, and being liable to be upset by economic, technological and productivity development. It seems probable, however, that, if the population were to grow by natural increase alone, in the Region as a whole there would be fewer persons of working age than at present. Taking into account migration trends also, however, it seems that there will be slightly more workers of both sexes available for employment.

---

* The Census of Production provides data of value added by the process of production and this is available for the old North Midland region for 1958. Similar data will be published in the 1963 Census of Production results for the reconstructed East Midlands Region; it is expected that such data will be available in the latter part of 1969.

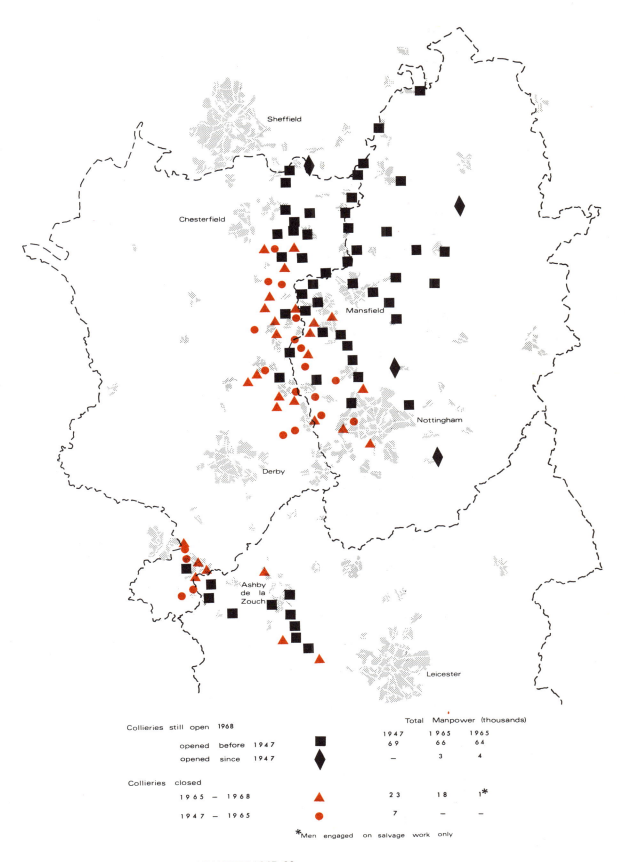

		Total	Manpower	(thousands)
Collieries still open 1968		1947	1965	1965
opened before 1947	■	69	66	64
opened since 1947	◆	—	3	4
Collieries closed				
1965 — 1968	▲	2 3	1 8	1*
1947 — 1965	●	7	—	—

*Men engaged on salvage work only

Fig. 6. EAST MIDLANDS COAL INDUSTRY 1947-68

The diagram shows changes in collieries and employment since 1947.

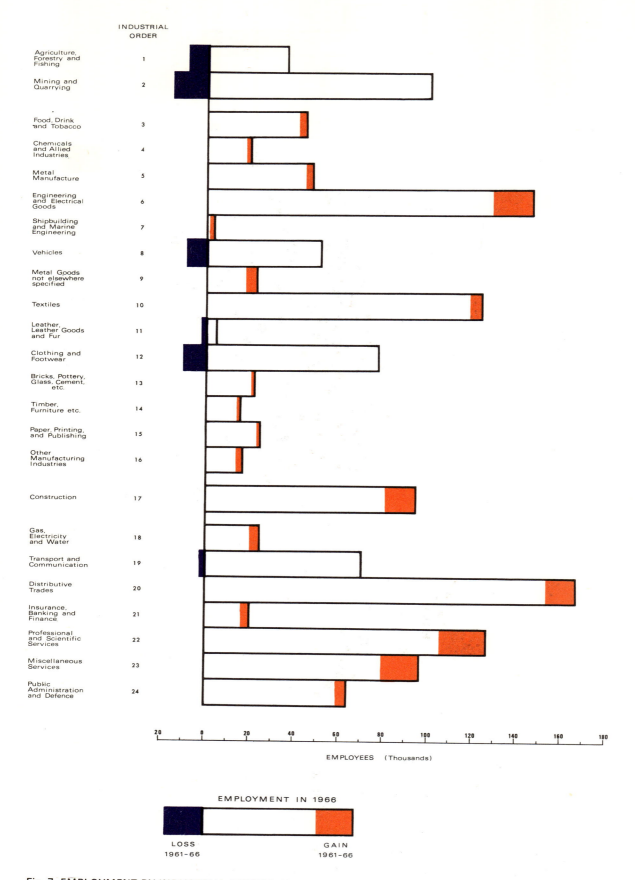

Fig. 7. EMPLOYMENT BY INDUSTRIAL ORDERS 1966 AND CHANGES 1961-66

The lengths of the columns represent the number of employees in employment in 1966 in each industrial order of the Standard Industrial Classification.
See Appendix 5.

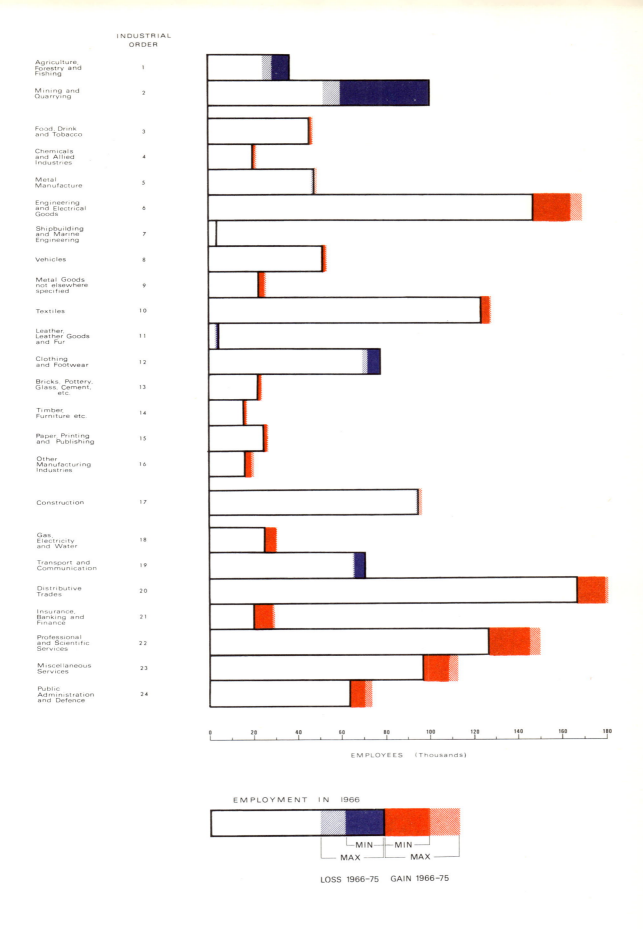

Fig. 8. EMPLOYMENT BY INDUSTRIAL ORDERS 1966 AND CHANGES 1966-75

The lengths of the columns represent the number of employees in employment in 1966 in each industrial order of the Standard Industrial Classification. The coloured areas indicate the forecast minimum and maximum changes 1966-75.

54.   As far as jobs for these workers are concerned, reference has already been made to the inevitable decline in employment for men in coalmining and agriculture. It is anticipated that there will be little change in the construction industry, but that more jobs will be available in the manufacturing and service industries. In manufacturing, the largest increases for men and women are expected to occur in engineering and electrical goods. The service industries as a group, however, have shown the greatest overall growth rate in the last few years (11.9% between 1961 and 1966, compared with 3.7% for the manufacturing group in the same period) and it is this group which is likely to supply the greatest number of extra jobs. Most of these are likely to be for women but service industries are nevertheless expected to provide about as many extra jobs for men as are manufacturing industries.

55.   The result is likely to be a rough balance in supply and demand for males in the Region as a whole, although this assumes that additional new jobs will arise in those parts of the Region, such as Northamptonshire, which are likely to receive a large proportion of inward migration. It is likely, however, that there will be a surplus of male workers in those areas of the Nottinghamshire/ Derbyshire sub-region where coalmining redundancies are concentrated. The demand for female workers is likely to outstrip the supply. Broadly speaking, with these two reservations, economic development is not likely to be critically hampered by a manpower shortage or to result in a reduced demand for men and women of working age.

56.   In this endeavour to clarify the economic prospects and contribution of the Region, the export position also has been studied. Whilst there are no regional export statistics available and one cannot quantify the contribution made by East Midlands industry in this field, the Region's export achievements are nevertheless known to be very significant. Seventeen Queen's Awards for Industry have already been won by firms in the Region for their export achievements. In fact, the diversified East Midlands economy has a strong representation of many of the industries prominent in the export trade. We welcome the requirement under the new company legislation that companies publish their export turnover figures as part of their annual report.

57.   The engineering group of industries is very important in the Region, providing approximately 33% of the Region's employment in manufacturing. Of particular note in this sector are aircraft engines, textile machinery, contractors' plant and cycles. The traditional industries, hosiery and footwear, also make a very useful contribution to exports. In terms of employees the Region accounts for approximately 60% of the hosiery industry and 44% of the footwear industry. During 1967 the country's footwear exports totalled £20 million (7% of output), whilst hosiery exports amounted to £32.5 million (13% of output). Other important sectors include metal tubes, pharmaceutical and scientific instruments. A survey of some 50 major manufacturing companies in the Region suggests that they alone contributed in 1965 something like £170 million of exports, or about 4½% of total manufacturing exports that year.

58.   In this chapter prominence has been given to the significance of the engineering group of industries for the future prospects of employment in the Region. Our confidence in these prospects is derived as much from the consideration of likely output requirements as of productivity improvements and labour supply. These output requirements will involve massive increases in the longer term if the national economy is to sustain a satisfactory growth rate. The engineering group of industries provides the machinery and plant basic to industrial expansion for the full range of production to meet home and overseas demand. The scale required for the export sector is indicated by the fact that over the period 1958-1967 the engineering group nationally has contributed consistently nearly 45% of the country's exports (by value) and that over the same period exports, as a whole, have increased at an annual rate of about 4½%.

59.   As suggested in paragraph 55, it is not possible to be confident about the Region's ability to absorb the run-down in mining manpower. This is likely to be on a larger scale, and with larger individual units affected than in the case of the other industries. Moreover the location of present employment is on average further from the possible alternatives, and some of the manpower, because of age or disability, tends to be less versatile. East Derbyshire is already particularly badly affected, and it seems probable that the Worksop locality of north Nottinghamshire will also

Rockingham village.

Full fashion knitting machines being assembled at
the factory of William Cotton Ltd., Loughborough,
the world's largest builder of such machines.

give rise to employment difficulties. But even when alternative employment for both the present and future generations can be found within commuting distance, there will still be a likelihood of a slow run-down of the existing communities unless replacement industry can be located more conveniently.

60.   There are other areas, Lincoln and the Lincolnshire towns, and parts of Northamptonshire and Leicestershire, where the existing industrial base is very specialised and therefore vulnerable both to the long-term changes outlined above and to the more specific difficulties occurring at any time, but which are uncomfortably far from any alternative source of employment when such difficulties arise.

61.   The Region is unlikely to have any problem in meeting its needs for power. The coal, gas and electricity industries are likely to be able to meet any demand, subject only to the proviso that they are given sufficient warning of the location of major developments to organise the distribution system.

62.   It has, however, to be recognised that the position of the Region as a powerhouse for the country was largely based on the conjunction of coal and the Trent. While existing policies on oil tax and preference for coal continue and coal remains a competitive source of fuel for the generation of electricity, the newer generating stations will remain of great importance, though the use of the older ones will diminish as time passes. If electricity for other parts of the country begins from the mid-1970s to be supplied from more local oil-fired or nuclear powered generating stations, the economic gain to the Region resulting from the present scale of coal-fired generation may well be reduced.

63.   The rapid influx of North Sea gas will be a benefit to the Region in the long run despite the heavy cost of the conversions essential to its use. Its technical and amenity advantages are evident and we welcome the Government's efforts to bring about its rapid development, even though the Region may lose some of the economic advantage it has had from the cheapness of its coal supply relative to other regions.

64.   We therefore forsee over the next fifteen to thirty years a reduction in the relative importance of the traditional labour-intensive industries and a considerable development of the newer capital-intensive industries. We regard this not only as inevitable but to be welcomed, as most likely to provide a basis for a faster rising standard of life. With this, or in its train, will come a further development of service industries, directed both to assisting the manufacturing sector and to enriching the life of the individual.

65.   We are very conscious that these long-term trends will present a continuing series of problems - industrial, local and personal - which we, in common with all the other organs of society, must meet and, where possible, anticipate in effective action. Action which we believe will contribute to a solution of these problems is considered further in the next chapter.

CHAPTER 4

The implementation of a regional strategy

66. The difficulties which will inevitably arise during the course of the considerable changes foreshadowed in the earlier chapters will be greatly reduced if government and other public agencies are ready and prepared to adjust policies to meet the developing situation.

67. Regional strategy must include the identification of places or areas which should accommodate growth both of population and industry. Public policies, together or separately, can do no more than influence the total social dynamic though, in some cases, as with local authority planning and industrial development certificate policy, this influence will be important. Regional strategy will modify a situation where change, in terms of growth, decline or substitution of one basis for another, will be taking place in response to innumerable private decisions.

68. Progress in regional development is closely linked with investment decisions in both the public and private sectors. In the public sector, expenditure on capital formation is particularly important in relation to regional development because of its effect on the infrastructure of the regions and its contribution towards their economic growth. By far the greater proportion of this expenditure arises as a result of programmes for which local and other public authorities are executively responsible, even though a very substantial proportion of the cost is met by government grants or loans and the level of the programme is subject to central control. The Regional Planning Councils were created to advise the Government on the regional implications of national policies, including the regional considerations which apply to the Government's proposals for future public investment on new building and construction. The Government has to formulate national priorities for such things as houses, roads, schools, universities and hospitals and the Planning Council has to examine the pattern of investment proposals for the region and advise on future regional priorities. The advice of Regional Economic Planning Councils on timing and emphasis should, as soon as they have gone far enough in their long-term planning, make a valuable contribution to decisions. Some differences of view are inevitable and the problems they pose are very far from being resolved but it is expected that, in the discussions about such differences, the Government's objective of ensuring that programmes become more closely geared to regional needs will be furthered.

69. Industrial development in every part of the country is greatly influenced by the Government's location of industry policy, and in particular by the restraints imposed by the need for industrial development certificates. In the past this Region has attracted industry from other regions - for example, into the new and expanding towns of Northamptonshire. At the same time it has made a substantial contribution to the generation of industry and creation of jobs which have been steered to development areas. At the beginning of 1968 the post-war moves of manufacturing industry from the East Midlands known to the Board of Trade were providing approximately 47,000 jobs in other parts of the country, including some 37,800 jobs in the development areas and Northern Ireland. Some of these firms were also known to have expansion schemes in hand which could provide a further 12,000 jobs, of which 10,000 were associated with extensions to units in the development areas. We accept that in present circumstances this policy must substantially continue. We recognise that there has been some modification in its immediate application but we ask that it should be progressively revised and modified as the differences in economic opportunity between different areas of the country are diminished.

70.   The primary object of location of industry policy is to reduce the disparity between employment opportunities - achieving all the social and economic advantages that this reduction would bring - but the present division of the country into development areas and non-development areas, and the public presentation of statistics, tend to hide the fact that there are stretches within non-development areas where the position is comparable with that in parts of the development areas.

71.   We still consider, as we have affirmed orally and in writing to the Hunt Committee, that projects which could be steered short distances within a region from areas of relative prosperity into areas which are experiencing or are actively threatened with increasing unemployment should not be denied industrial development certificates for these latter areas.

72.   We are hopeful that our attempts to obtain government recognition of the Erewash Valley as an intermediate area needing some form of government assistance will be successful. The area would thus become more attractive to new or expanding industry and unemployment arising from the rundown of coalmining would be reduced. New job opportunities for school-leavers, whose traditional employment opportunities no longer exist, would also be provided.

73.   In the longer term we regard it as probable that the development areas - or most of them - will have ceased to depend so greatly on the heavy and declining industries, and that there will be room for a general modification of policy. In 1950 the manpower in mining, shipbuilding and agriculture in Scotland, Wales and the Northern Region together amounted to over 767,000; by 1959 this was down to 706,000 and by 1966 to 466,000. It is still true that those areas face serious problems as the decline continues, but their dependence on these industries is much less marked than it was and the achievement of a new equilibrium can at least be foreshadowed, though much will depend upon the successful pursuit of development area policies. The capital-intensive and science-based industries expand the fastest, and therefore bring themselves within the ambit of government steering policy. There is a danger that the indefinite continuation of present policies will deprive some non-development areas of a reasonable share of these industries. Despite the scale and diversity of new factory building which has taken place within the Region (*see* Table 4 and Appendices 6 and 7) the East Midlands, with a very heavy dependence on some traditional labour-intensive industries, is particularly exposed to this danger, and to the limitations on the general standard of life it would bring with it.

Table 4   East Midlands Region factories built 1962-67 with industrial development certificate approval.
Proportion of floorspace in each Industrial Order.

S.I.C. Order		Percentage
III.	Food, drink and tobacco	6
V.	Metal manufacture	17
VI.	Electrical and engineering	20
VIII.	Vehicles	5
X.	Textiles	13
XIII.	Bricks, pottery and glass	15
XIV.	Timber, furniture, etc.	5
XV.	Paper, printing and publishing	5
Remainder of Manufacturing Sectors : Orders IV, VII, IX, XI, XII and XVI		14
		100

74.   We regard it as necessary to ask that the Board of Trade - as the Department responsible for administering government policy in this field - should take fully into account the views of Economic Planning Councils as to the needs and potentialities of particular areas, not only for industry in general but for particular types of industry. We accept that the decisions on individual cases must remain a Board of Trade responsibility, and that the grounds for such decisions, involving matters of commercial confidence, cannot be revealed. The criteria used to determine the needs of an area should not, in our view, be so protected, since they are the legitimate concern of the local community; they should be determined openly after consultation with Economic Planning Councils, and take into account any local circumstances which may be put forward. Economic Planning Councils will need moreover to be kept informed about the nature and pace of economic expansion taking place, as related to the assessment of needs.

75.   We are conscious that the Board of Trade, in administering a policy which inevitably frustrates the desires and ambitions of some people, and doing so in the light of information which it receives and must retain in confidence, is in a difficult position, and we pay tribute to the thoroughness and impartiality it shows. The second function of Economic Planning Councils is 'to study and advise on the development of a long-term planning strategy for their regions on the basis of information and assessments provided by the Economic Planning Boards.' Much of this information will necessarily come from the Board of Trade and we trust that that Department will continue to provide all available information which is not barred by considerations of commercial confidence.

76.   Voluntary industrial movement will only take place if it is judged likely to increase total profitability, and even then may be inhibited by shorter-term considerations. Movement itself is expensive; it involves a dislocation which not all firms could stand, and to install technically up-to-date plant, however desirable, may be beyond the financial resources available, or the price may be high enough to destroy the marginal balance in favour of a move. Where such a move would serve a social as well as a business purpose, there is a case for society to meet some of the immediate costs. In principle, the case is the same as that accepted for investment grants in development areas; the urgency of need is very much less, and both the scale and methods of administration may well be different. It is, however, very possible that without some such aid the immobility of industry will frustrate both the replanning of our physical environment and its own modernisation.

77.   The relative immobility of industry underlies much of the criticism of i.d.c. decisions. However well they understand the general desirability of steering industry to development areas, local authorities elsewhere are bound to be disappointed when they see a possible industrial expansion or movement thwarted, knowing both that it would fit very well into well-considered plans for their own localities, and that the opportunity will be unlikely to recur for a long time. Under existing legislation, any large group having establishments in both development and non-development areas will tend to be drawn towards concentrating investment and expansion in the former.

78.   Given the knowledge of new technologies, and a willingness by industrialists to invest in them, it still remains necessary for individual localities to persuade those industrialists that they are the right places, and for the central government to be satisfied that investment in those places should be allowed. The East Midlands as a whole has great advantages - though the labour situation may be a limiting factor.

79.   It is not, therefore, only national policies in relation to industrial location which need to be reviewed. Some local authorities can, in their approach, be over-concerned with their own particular area, whether by over-providing industrial sites with inadequate consideration of what their neighbours are doing, or by adjusting their detailed planning to avoid the necessity for firms to move out of their area - even though only just across a boundary. However, we welcome the much greater degree of co-operation and consultation which has recently been evident. We are glad to note that the Town and Country Planning Act 1968 seeks as one of its main aims to secure the co-ordinated preparation and submission of new-style development plans for meaningful areas. The Act will also, by freeing central government from the local detail with which it has been

involved, enable it to concentrate more on the broad strategy issues. The relevance of the findings of the Royal Commission on Local Government - whatever they prove to be - to these problems is obvious, but at this stage it is impossible to go further.

80.   Although some movement of industry out of the most congested areas is desirable, the present capital investment in our towns is enormous and must be used rather than sacrificed. There would be no point in regarding location policies as directed primarily to dispersal - this would be economic folly. Both industry and the organisation of urban areas require units big enough to support variety of opportunity, and public transport systems large enough to be viable. Yet the pattern of towns and villages we have inherited will need modification to suit the economic and demographic situation which is developing, and methods of ensuring that these modifications are planned rather than haphazard must be found.

81.   Nevertheless these changes and those envisaged in Chapter 3 will clearly also require some new mobility, in terms of area and of occupation, on the part of the labour force. Labour immobility cannot be entirely removed, but adequate financial help to the individuals on the one hand and attractive amenities in the receiving areas on the other will reduce it.

82.   Mobility of workers as between different occupations is equally difficult. It is no longer possible to say to the majority of school-leavers that they can be trained in a particular occupation and expect to be employed in it for the whole of their working lives. Industry is therefore faced with training and re-training problems on an ever-increasing scale. The Industrial Training Boards have a vital role to play in tackling these problems.

83.   Local education authorities and industrial organisations are co-operating to arrange for teachers and senior pupils to get some personal experience of industry and for industrial managers to become acquainted with modern educational practices. We welcome these steps, which should help to ease the transition from school to industry and reduce the waste of effort in both fields which has resulted in the past from lack of contact between them.

84.   The right conditions for technological progress not only include the formal institutional frame-work of universities, research associations and the research and development departments of large businesses but also depend on the informal interchange of ideas among those brought close together in the first place by the proximity of these institutions. Science and technology are international, but some of the advantages are regional or local, because they depend on the informal rather than the formal exchanges. As is widely recognised, London and the south-east have hitherto enjoyed an obvious primacy - perhaps a near monopoly - in this respect. The situation appears slowly to be changing as the newer universities and newer industries develop together in other locations. The future vigour of the regions will depend in no small degree in fostering this type of development in their midst.

85.   We note with interest the efforts of the Regional Advisory Committee for Further Education in co-operation with the universities to organise courses of high quality in managerial techniques. We are convinced that constant attention to keeping management abreast of current developments will be required.

86.   The rise in productivity per head which is needed can only be secured by industry itself, and trade associations and research bodies within industry are alive to the need. Inter-firm comparison and consultancy services are increasingly used and mention too must be made of the promotional work of the British Productivity Council through its Regional Offices and district associations. Public authorities can help by providing facilities for research in some fields and for the dissemination of knowledge at all levels of industry in others. They also provide the communications and transport facilities which a modern industrial economy requires, and the environment which will make the efforts of management and employees alike seem worthwhile. It is here that good planning can support the efforts on which it in turn depends.

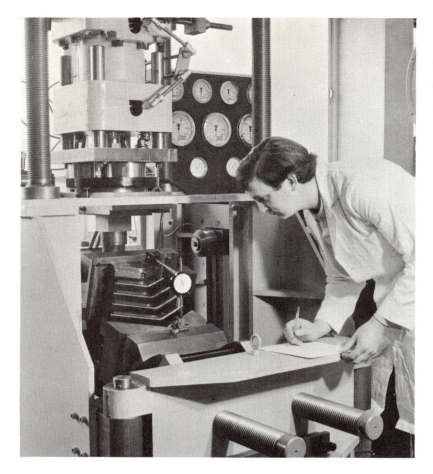

Checking the stiffness of
'Metalastik' rubber-
bonded-to-metal railway
axlebox springs in the
Research Laboratory of
the Dunlop Polymer
Engineering Division,
Leicester.

RB 211 engine on test.

87.   The Ministry of Technology has already developed within the Region a variety of services to assist firms in improving their productivity and technological awareness. Industrial Liaison Centres have been established in Nottingham, Derby, Northampton and Leicester to help the smaller firms to solve technological problems and to make better use of existing scientific and technical knowledge and further education facilities. Automation Centres have been established in Leicester and Nottingham to give instruction and advice to firms in the use of automation techniques. The Centres include laboratories equipped with commercially available automation aids and instructional films. A mobile unit of the Production Engineering Advisory Service, operated for the Ministry by the Production Engineering Research Association, is available to visit firms in the Region.

88.   Keeping pace with technical developments requires the use of capital resources. We would have wished to see the United Kingdom join the European Economic Community to ensure a market large enough to give an appropriate return on the capital investment required. Even in present circum- stances, closer economic co-operation with the Community seems desirable and probable. Mean- while the development of our partnership in the European Free Trade Association is unquestionably right for the best long-term interests of the country. Import saving is important to the balance of payments and for the East Midlands the position of agriculture, hosiery and footwear is of particular interest in this respect. However, the primary objective must be the achievement of an export boom as vanguard to a satisfactory growth rate for the national economy, and the Government offers industry many services which should directly or indirectly improve export performance. Some of these are described in Appendix 9.

89.   Exporting experience in the East Midlands in recent years strongly reflects the national tendency to make wider and more intelligent use of the services of government departments. During 1967 several hundred of the Region's exporting firms - totalling more than 2,500 at the last count - took part in overseas exhibitions, trade fairs, British Weeks and store promotions in collaboration with the Board of Trade's overseas specialists. East Midlands representation in these events covered 42 countries and 30 separate manufacturing industries. Leicester and County Chamber of Commerce has, since 1962, mounted nearly 30 trade missions to some 30 countries and has organised local participation in 7 British Weeks and Samples Displays abroad. Export orders directly resulting were conservatively estimated at £6½ million to end 1968. Northampton and Nottingham are also exploring the possibilities of trade missions to augment the results of the strongly individual approaches to exporting and have sent missions to Scandinavia and the U.S.S.R. Another healthy sign is the growth of clubs and discussion groups designed to stimulate interest in the export trade. Nottingham led the way with the formation in March, 1966 of its Export Association, since developed into an active and purposeful organisation. Common to all of them is the desire not merely to improve export performance but to improve the standards of professionalism in selling abroad. Being conscious of the paramount importance of exports we welcome any effort designed to increase the scope and efficiency of the East Midlands' performance in this vital area.

90.   We also consider that more attention should be paid to the structure of industry and the creation of more efficient units which can command the necessary capital. We regard this as particularly important in the East Midlands, where the number of small units in the traditional industries may impose some limitations on modernisation. This is not to suggest, of course, that there are not within the Region many businesses of all sizes with a lively tradition of technological change and the most up-to-date plant.

91.   The rationalisation of industry is continuing within the Region. The activities of Courtaulds Ltd. and Viyella International have already made a great impact in the textile industry. In vehicle manufacture the Leyland-B.M.H. merger may have repercussions. Internal re-organisation within the English Electric Co. had led to the closure of Alfred Wiseman & Co. Ltd. in Grantham. It is too early to forsee the precise results of the A.E.I.-G.E.C. merger. Both firms had interests in the Region.

CHAPTER 5

Transport

GENERAL

92.   The need for improvements in transport facilities must be effectively anticipated, but rapid technological changes are taking place. Loughborough and Nottingham Universities are active in the field of hovercraft technology and an industry manufacturing small hovercraft is developing rapidly in this Region. A system of four-seater automatic cars to run on a special track to provide urban transport facilities is being actively developed at Loughborough with National Research Development Corporation backing. However, it is impossible to forecast which of the novel forms of transport now being subjected to research will be developed. Some may begin to make a contribution to urban transport later this century, but there is insufficient evidence as to their practicability for us to take them into account in our regional strategy.

93.   Even in conventional transport, with faster rail services, automatic control, use of containers, modernisation of ports, more efficient road vehicles and improved highway design, the rate of development is rapid. Road-borne commercial and industrial traffic will inevitably increase and adequate roads will be needed to carry it, but growing use of the private car must also be catered for as far as is possible. Also, changes will occur in residential and industrial concentrations, in the pattern of international trade and the roles of individual ports, and a further rapid increase in passenger and freight transport by air is expected. All these developments will call for changes in the patterns of inland transport.

94.   Sufficient information is already available to indicate the broad needs for transport facilities but in order to make the best use of the existing infrastructure and of the heavy investment which must in any case be put into its improvement over the next two decades, the growth of population and industry will have to be based on the existing transport network.

95.   The broad transport strategy falls into three parts. Firstly, to ensure that good links are available between the major centres of population and industry within the Region. Secondly, to ensure that there are good communications between the Region and the rest of the country, particularly to the London, Merseyside and Humberside ports and to Birmingham and the West Midlands. Thirdly, to ensure that the larger towns are provided with an efficient internal transport system so that economic and environmental losses through congestion and danger are reduced to a minimum.

Roads

96.   We reaffirm the importance of all the new links we called for in the East Midlands Study, and are pleased to learn that the Government has accepted the need for comprehensively improved routes from the Nottingham and Derby area to Birmingham and the south-west and to Manchester and the north-west. We note that the link from the southern part of the Region to the East Anglian ports (A45) is to be markedly improved over the next few years and we emphasise the importance to the development of the Region of the early completion of these improvements and the continued modernisation of this route.

97. Since we produced the Study the need for improved links to Humberside has become clearer. The projected motorway link from the Humber to join M18 and A1(M) in the Doncaster area will greatly benefit the northern part of our Region and provide an adequate route for those centres which are not far from M1. However, there is a growing volume of traffic, originating largely outside the Region, moving southwards across Lincolnshire and because of this it is important that a by-pass should be provided for Lincoln City and that the dualling of the Fosse Way (A46) should be completed as far south as Leicester as soon as possible. In the longer term it is likely that a further major north - south route to the east of A1 will be needed, possibly via route A15 to Peterborough, to relieve both A1 and Lincolnshire's inadequate road system.

98.   We must emphasise the Region's need for improved links from M1 to Sheffield, and recommend that this should be provided by a comprehensive improvement of routes A616 and A619 from Sheffield to Eckington, the Barlborough M1 interchange and Worksop. These routes are at present the responsibility of the local highway authorities, but we recommend that in view of their national importance consideration should be given to their forming part of the national road network. In addition, the whole of route A61 between Chesterfield and Sheffield should be improved.

99.   Despite the acceptance of our proposals for improved routes to the south-west and to the north-west of Nottingham, east-west communications still provide the Region with its biggest problem. In addition to the East Anglian route advocated above, the general improvement of route A52 between Nottingham, Grantham and Boston and of A17 to King's Lynn is of vital importance if the Eastern Lowlands are to be able to develop with the rest of the Region. We consider this route has more than a local significance and we recommend that it should be improved.

100. We have already said that the Erewash Valley should, in our opinion, be redeveloped. For this purpose good communications are essential and M1 is the key.   It has spare capacity which it would be wasteful not to use. With proper feeder routes the Valley should be very attractive to industry and the development of such feeder routes is, therefore, a major feature of the Region's strategy.

101. The roads which we recommend should receive priority treatment for development in this general area are :
    A610 Nottingham-Nuthall (M1)-Eastwood-Langley Mill-Ripley A61
    A615 Mansfield-Sutton-Pinxton (M1)-Alfreton A61
    A617 Mansfield-Heath (M1)-Chesterfield A61
    A61 from north of Alfreton to Derby
We are glad to note that sections of these routes are included for improvement either in the firm road programme or in schemes under preparation, but we emphasise the desirability of the early completion of the whole programme as detailed above, in order to provide an efficient transport infrastructure to the area at the earliest possible date.

102. Road access to East Midlands Airport from the east is via B5400 from Kegworth, a village on A6 with a number of traffic hazards. Proposals exist for a by-pass of the village from the M1/A6 interchange at Lockington to a point on B5400 west of Kegworth. This new route will greatly improve access to the airport and make an important contribution to the modernisation of the Region's transport system at relatively little cost. We recommend that the scheme should be put in hand quickly.

103. Corby has lost its rail passenger services, and most freight is likely to continue to travel by road. This is a prosperous area with a large element of private car ownership and the roads provide an important public transport link for Corby. If Corby is to attract industry from the South East, the A6003 road to Kettering and the south must be improved.

104. There has been much pressure for the improvement of A6 throughout Northamptonshire, as it passes through a series of towns all of which hamper the free flow of traffic. We are conscious that much of the traffic is of a local nature between the various towns and having business in them.

This means that by-passes, or a completely new route, would benefit only a proportion of traffic now using A6. However, the difficulties are likely to increase and we must record that there is a serious risk of development being retarded unless a new route on the line of A6 is opened up in the next decade.

105. As traffic increases, the special environment of towns of historic or architectural interest, and sometimes the structure of the buildings which give them their particular interest, is suffering. We are of the opinion that decisions on the need for road improvements to divert traffic from such areas should not be based solely on the usual traffic considerations but should take account also of the need to safeguard the heritage these towns represent. We hope that local authorities will use their powers under the Civic Amenities Act to designate suitable areas for conservation.

Railways

106. The basic network of railways which is to be developed meets, to a large extent, the needs of the Region. Development of the link from Northampton to the Leicester-Kettering line would incorporate Northampton in the network linking the Region's main centres. As with roads, however, rail communications with East Anglia are poor. They are via London, via Grantham and Peterborough or via Leicester, Melton Mowbray and Peterborough. We regard the Leicester-Peterborough-East Anglia route as of particular importance and would like to see services on it improved.

107. The Eastern Lowlands present a major problem. Their main link with Nottingham via Grantham has been in some danger of losing its passenger services. It provides an important link with the long distance East Coast route and should be retained for passengers. British Railways' plans would also lead to the complete isolation of Spalding. The closure proposals for the East Lincolnshire line from Peterborough through that town to Boston and Grimsby, and for the link from that line at Firsby to Lincoln would, if implemented, almost denude the Eastern Lowlands of passenger services. The retention of the East Lincolnshire line at least until satisfactory alternative public transport is available is of great importance to the area, and we have been impressed by the importance of maintaining passenger transport between Peterborough and Boston. The present highway system is inadequate and would be costly to improve; public passenger services in any area so lightly populated are likely to be inadequate unless they are in some way publicly subsidised.

Urban transport

108. Urban transport facilities must be improved and, despite continued heavy expenditure on roads, improvements in the public transport system will be required. Most commuters travel only short distances, so an increase in the use of conventional rail transport for commuting is unlikely. Buses, perhaps in places on reserved tracks and perhaps, ultimately, with automatic control over certain stages, are likely to play the major part in urban mass transport because of their flexibility. However, the Nottingham-Grantham line already mentioned provides one of our few commuter services. It links a number of growing settlements to both Nottingham and Grantham and its value for carrying commuters and shoppers to these main centres emphasises the need for its retention for passengers.

109. In general, the solution to the urban transport problem must rest with the local authorities. They have already produced development proposals for all the significant centres of population. The aim must be to improve the highway system whilst limiting the number of cars using it to conform to its capacity, and to make such provision for public transport vehicles that they become attractive because of their speed, regularity and cheapness. A major feature in any highway system must be the provision of adequate off-street parking and, in any transport plan, parking on at least major routes through built-up areas must be prohibited, so that the fullest use can be made of roads for traffic movement.

110. The maximum spread of the transport load must be sought in order to minimise the one-way peak traffic flows now jamming roads which at other times are under-utilised. Staggering of working hours, coupled with night or evening delivery to shops and industry, could bring enormous and

immediate benefits in reducing congestion. Staggering of hours is unpopular, and night delivery is expensive, but the benefits accruing from them require us to press for their introduction.

Ports
111. The Region has no major port. Its imports and exports will continue to move in the main through the Humber and Thames ports and Merseyside, with considerable flows through the East Anglian ports and through the Channel Tunnel in due course. The estuarial port areas of great interest to this Region are three of the terminals of the long distance axes on which the country is often expected to develop. These axes cross just to the west of our Region but communications along them are vital to us.

112. Boston, an important municipally owned port situated in a predominantly agricultural area but geographically close to the industrial areas of the East Midlands, is in our opinion suitable for development. We think that it has potential as a terminal for hovercraft services as these develop across the North Sea.

Waterways
113. The Trent carried about 20 million ton-miles of freight in 1967. It could carry more but expenditure of further substantial capital on its improvement cannot have a high priority in the Region's transport strategy.

Freight transport
114. The new goods licensing arrangements contained in the 1968 Transport Act will help the railways to compete for bulk and long distance traffic. Much of the Region's industry produces small parcels and road transport may be a more efficient carrier for such loads than is British Railways. However, the miscellaneous nature of the traffic emphasises the importance of containers, and the National Freight Corporation which took over the railways sundries and freight liner services on 1st January, 1969 should be well placed to handle the movement of the products of the Region's industry to home and export markets. In addition to the freight liner depot associated with an inland clearance depot at Nottingham, a similar arrangement in Northampton and a freight liner depot at Peterborough to serve south Lincolnshire are essential for efficient goods transport, whilst depots in Leicester and Lincoln are highly desirable.

Passenger transport
115. If the growth in the use of private cars continues at the present rate, it may not be possible to keep pace with the growth in traffic congestion, despite any reduction that might be achieved by the removal of some traffic generators from congested areas. Within our towns we must therefore encourage the public transport operators to provide services which offer an attractive and acceptable alternative to private transport. If more people could be encouraged to use public transport it would reduce congestion on the roads and, if a real breakthrough could be achieved, could lead to a reduction in the ever growing demand for greater expenditure on our road network, to the benefit of other important elements in the Region's infrastructure.

116. This Region seems unlikely to have a Passenger Transport Authority yet awhile. We see the theoretical advantages of these near monopolies and strongly support arguments that there should be the closest possible liaison between all the Planning and Transport Authorities. By co-operation they could achieve much of what is expected from formally constituted authorities on the lines proposed for the major conurbations. In any case, the East Midlands, with its free-standing urban areas, poses different problems from the main conurbations. Rural areas, of which we have many, are the least financially attractive for public transport, and it is just these areas where improvements are most needed which may not lend themselves readily to incorporation in Passenger Transport Authorities. Adequate services may call for subsidies way beyond the means of the relatively poor local authorities involved and we welcome the proposals for a government contribution of 50% of such subsidies.

Pipelines

117. With North Sea gas off our coast much attention is being given to pipelines. Apart from gas, petroleum products are the main substances for which pipelines are used. We consider that this means of transportation should be more fully exploited and pipelines used to convey as wide a range of commodities as possible.

Air transport

118. We attach great importance to the further development of the East Midlands Airport at Castle Donington. A primary interest of the Region is the development of fast, regular and convenient services to major centres on the continent of Europe. In general, existing services are inconvenient to the East Midlands and difficulty of access to the London airports in particular materially reduces the speed advantage which air transport should bring.

119. The absence of national decisions on the role of individual airports makes the development of a coherent system of air transport slower and more difficult. We believe that the East Midlands Airport should be accepted as a developing international airport and that air licensing authorities should reach decisions on individual applications in the light of that acceptance. We note that the regional importance of air services is one of the things the Edwards Committee of Inquiry into Civil Air Transport is looking at and we look forward to its recommendations on the development of services from regional airports.

Transport for exports

120. If the Region is to increase its already important contribution to the export drive it must have good links with the growing export markets - especially Europe and North America, which are likely to be major growth sectors, although the traditional trade with sterling and Commonwealth countries elsewhere can be expected to remain massive and to grow. It is an inland workshop and its export industries must take advantage of the inland clearance and container systems, including freight liner and roll-on/roll-off services, for transport through the modernised berths at the ports. Apart from the major estuarial port areas mentioned above, we need another outlet orientated towards Denmark, the Low Countries and the European Economic Community, and we hope that Boston will be able to develop to meet some of this need.

121. For the immediate future, the Felixstowe/Ipswich/Harwich complex offers the best facilities, existing and potential, although at a considerable distance from the Region's major centres. A45 from Northampton to Ipswich is being improved and we have pressed for more to be done quickly. However, the great opportunity here seems to be in bulking small consignments at inland clearance depots and freight liner terminals for rail haulage to link with shipping services, such as the container-ship service now operated by British Rail from Harwich. Felixstowe has the added advantage of being able to handle ships of substantial size at all states of the tide, and we look forward to the early linking of all three port areas with the freight liner network.

122. For really urgent consignments the East Midlands Airport, situated near the industrial heart of the Region and with potentially good road communications, is the key. Within a decade, we foresee it being a major outlet for other exports, including commodities which are not yet thought of as suitable for air transport. It offers the Region important and developing facilities in an industry which is growing faster than almost any other and which we consider must continue to expand rapidly for the benefit of the export trades.

CHAPTER 6

The physical environment

HOUSING

123. The adjustments to the population forecasts which were explained in Chapter 2 do not seriously affect the conclusions reached in the East Midlands Study on the needs of the Region in the fields of housing and water supplies. In the Study, the Region's average yearly requirement for new houses was estimated as 27,500 for the period 1965-81; this was compared with 22,300 completions in 1965 and the conclusion was that although completions would have to be stepped up, the satisfaction by 1981 of the known needs was not impracticable. It has been suggested that the target cannot be achieved by normal methods and present resources and that a more rationalised and industrial approach to building must be applied to large-scale schemes. There is no doubt that improved efficiency in the building industry and more prefabrication of components would help, and the search for these improvements will be a continuing process. But the scope for industrialised housing, in the full sense of preconstructed buildings merely assembled on site, is rather limited; except in the case of very large developments or high-rise flats the more traditional methods (including rationalised traditional) are usually cheaper. High-rise flats are not regarded with favour, except for some limited and local circumstances. The advantages of fully industrialised building are not likely, therefore, to make a serious contribution - except perhaps for the very large development expected at Northampton - but there is no indication that the building industry will not be able to cope with a continued increase in the housing programme. We think it important however that, in dealing with the problems of housing or re-housing large numbers of people, local authorities should encourage awareness of visual amenity and lead the way in preserving or improving the overall environment, which is too easily damaged by the effect of unimaginative development, particularly at very high residential density.

124. Recent review of the estimates in the East Midlands Study has shown fluctuations in various factors, e.g., transfer of Mosbrough to Sheffield, change in family formation estimates, increase in planned overspill in Northamptonshire and shortfall for the first two years of the period averaged. Taken together (and bearing in mind that some of the changes were based on a 10% sample census) these changes fall within the possible margin of error likely in the published assessment. The position shown in the East Midlands Study is given in Table 5 on the following page.

Table 5   Dwellings: Yearly Completions, 1956-65 and Yearly Need, 1965-81

	Completions			Average Yearly Need 1965-81
	Yearly Average 1956-65	1964	1965	
East Midlands Sub-Regions:	20,100	22,900	22,300	27,500
Nottinghamshire/ Derbyshire	10,200	11,500	11,100	15,000
Leicester	4,700	4,900	5,000	4,000
Eastern Lowlands	2,300	2,900	2,800	3,000
Northamptonshire	2,900	3,600	3,400	5,500

The progress made can be seen from the following table.

Table 6   Dwellings: Completions 1966 and 1967

	1966			1967		
	L.A. and other public	Private	Total	L.A. and other public	Private	Total
East Midlands Sub-Regions:	6,723	17,358	24,081	9,223	15,885	25,108
Nottinghamshire/ Derbyshire	3,546	7,384	10,930	5,428	6,779	12,207
Leicester	1,124	4,425	5,549	996	4,078	5,074
Eastern Lowlands	984	2,687	3,671	1,058	2,491	3,549
Northamptonshire	1,069	2,862	3,931	1,741	2,537	4,278

Sub-Regional variations

125. These tables show that when current completion rates are related to the estimated average yearly needs there are wide variations between the sub-regions in the East Midlands. It is not necessary for completions for each year to meet the average. For example, the total need for Northamptonshire of 88,000 includes 50,000 for growth of new and expanding towns, but year by year progress depends on many factors and the appropriate rate is related to these, not to averages. Because of the special circumstances in Northamptonshire, the overall position in the Region can be expressed more clearly by taking this area separately:

	Average Yearly Need	Completions 1966	1967
Northamptonshire	5,500	3,931	4,278
Rest of Region	22,000	20,150	20,830

The shortfall in the Northamptonshire sub-region amounts to nearly 2,000 houses per year, However, as explained above, the figure for Northamptonshire includes 50,000 households (i.e. average of 3,100 per year) arising from the planned growth of Corby, Daventry, Northampton and

A line of heel nailing machines being built.

Low rise housing in Corby at 16 dwellings to the acre — awarded the Ministry of Housing and Local Government Gold Medal for Good Design in Housing 1966.

Wellingborough. Completions in respect of planned growth in these towns amounted to less than 800 in 1966 and about 1,400 in 1967. The present programme appears to be running at a reasonable level to meet the indigenous needs of Northamptonshire but will have to be stepped up by about 1,700 houses a year to provide for the planned growth. Possibly 1,000 of these will need to be built by public authorities. All of this must be dependent on the rate of industrial build-up being adequate to provide employment for the increase of population this rate of house-building implies.

Public and private building

126. The tables also reveal a considerable difference for the sub-regions as between houses provided for letting by public bodies and those built primarily for owner-occupation. The Leicester and Eastern Lowlands sub-regions, because of the high proportion of private housing, are running ahead of estimated average annual need. The total current programme for these two sub-regions appears to be running at a satisfactory rate overall. The most serious discrepancy between current completions and estimated yearly need arises in the Nottinghamshire/Derbyshire sub-region. Completion rates show that private enterprise building is running at about half of the total estimated average yearly need, although private development has not been restricted by shortage of housing land or the capacity of the building industry. The rate of completions can therefore be taken as nearly satisfying the effective demand for newly-built private houses, and the difference between that and the average yearly need represents the shortage of local authority provision. On this basis the Nottinghamshire/Derbyshire sub-region requires an annual completion rate of about 8,000 local authority houses.

127. Even after taking account of not less than 4,000 re-lets each year from existing stock, the general housing need cannot in fact be satisfied without additional provision by local authorities. In the industrial towns of the East Midlands (and particularly in the Nottinghamshire/Derbyshire sub-region's industrial zone) there will be a continuing requirement for houses to rent which, in practice, must nearly all be provided by local authorities. In Northamptonshire the programme will have to be increased to provide for planned migration. The greatest increase, however, should occur in the Nottinghamshire/Derbyshire sub-region to ensure that the total average yearly need is met.

128. Paragraph 264 of the Study referred to the relatively high ratio of private enterprise houses to local authority houses built in the Region. The subsequent slight change in this ratio has been brought about by the increased housing programmes of a few local authorities who are faced with formidable tasks in clearing unfit houses.

129. Assessments made by local housing authorities have confirmed the view expressed in the Study that, in some areas, the existing stock of local authority rented houses is already large enough virtually to meet the demand for such housing. This is most marked in parishes and towns where the population has declined or remained static over the last twenty years. In other areas, particularly where population has increased and there are a considerable number of obsolete dwellings, a serious housing problem remains. The public sector housing programme should be concentrated on those areas where the need is greatest.

130. Conditions will not remain constant throughout the period up to 1981 but we recommend that the annual programme for public authority house building in each sub-region up to 1975 should be:

Nottinghamshire/Derbyshire	8,500
Leicester	1,000
Eastern Lowlands	1,000
Northamptonshire	2,000

The public authority house building programmes for periods after 1975 will need to be reviewed in the light of progress made by, say, 1972. Of course, much depends on the part played by the private enterprise sector in the provision of new houses. This will depend on demand by individuals and even with government encouragement by way of 100 per cent option mortgages, etc., the scope for personal decision makes it impossible to estimate private enterprise completions beyond a year or so in advance.

Unfit houses

131. Over the whole Region, the rate of clearing unfit houses remains far below that estimated in Table 12 of the East Midlands Study. Of the average yearly need of 27,500 houses shown in Table 5 12,500 are required for replacement of houses which may be regarded as unfit. Against this yearly need of 12,500, only 4,142 were demolished or closed in 1966 and only 4,366 in 1967. On this basis it would take about eleven years to clear all the houses which local authorities have provisionally classed as unfit.

132. In 1966 and 1967 49,200 houses were completed in the Region, a net increase of about 40,700 houses. This is far in excess of the additional need for houses which will have accrued during the period, and will have reduced the overall shortage, which the Study estimated to be 28,000 in 1965. As the shortage is overtaken, slum clearance will gain momentum. Except in certain difficult areas, the backlog of unfit houses should be cleared by 1974. In the White Paper *Old Houses into New Homes (Cmnd. 3602)* the Government proposed that sound houses lacking modern amenities should be improved, together with their environment, and conserved. Before 1974 this policy should reduce the annual flow of houses becoming unfit and by 1981 the housing needs of the Region should be being met as they arise.

133. This policy of conserving sound houses could mean that the replacement need estimated in the Study at 200,000 was over-assessed. The proposed policy should extend the useful life of the sounder houses but its implementation would be no justification for extending the life of houses which are beyond being improved and conserved. We see no reason to reduce the average yearly replacement need from the 12,500 given in the Study. Even if, out of the Study estimate of 200,000 houses in need of replacement, there are only 75,000 houses which cannot be improved, these would take six years to clear at the rate we suggest. We believe this estimate to be on the low side and are conscious that each 12,500 by which it falls short of the true figure adds a further year to the length of time needed to get rid of them.

WATER

134. We note with satisfaction that our warnings about future difficulties on water supply have been taken seriously, and that considerable investment is in hand in the area of the Tame Valley to improve the quality of effluent discharged into tributaries of the Trent. The relative proportions of natural flow and sewage effluent are so abnormal that, apart from the need for new and improved sewage disposal facilities, further consideration of the problems is clearly needed. We are therefore very glad that the Water Resources Board and the River Authority are co-operating on a special study. This should provide an answer on the economic production of potable water from the river. If the study shows this to be feasible, it may also show the need for a new approach to the definitions of quality of effluents discharged into the river. It seems improbable that the required volume and quality of water can be provided without very heavy capital expenditure. We are of the opinion that estimates of demand tend to be accepted uncritically and that more attention should be paid to the relationship between demand and price for water.

135. The problems of water supply in the southern and eastern areas of the Region are less pressing than those of the north, but since these areas are naturally drier it is necessary to look further ahead to ensure that action is taken in good time. We are therefore pleased that a desk study of the Wash barrage scheme is being undertaken and we hope that if its outcome is favourable a full feasibility study will follow quickly. We accept that similar studies in other estuaries may throw light on problems in the Wash but, even so, the delay may have serious consequences to the development of middle England in due course.

136. In general, we hope that the present reliance on flooding large acreages, whether of high quality agricultural land or land with high scenic and amenity value, will be reviewed in the light of the programmes of research and costing undertaken by the Water Resources Board and other authorities and will, if possible, be curtailed. It is appreciated however that, until alternative

methods are fully available, it may still be necessary to proceed as before with the provision of new reservoirs, because the demand doubles every twenty years and it takes something like ten years to plan and complete a reservoir.

PHYSICAL AMENITY

137. In the field of physical planning we emphasise the need for good environment and amenity. The Region has large areas of parkland, including part of the Peak National Park, the Dukeries and Sherwood Forest parklands, Charnwood Forest and the parks in the larger towns, such as the 450-acre Wollaton Park in Nottingham. Parts of these and other areas, such as Elvaston Castle Estate near Derby, are being developed as country parks. The Region abounds in opportunities for water recreation. Its coastline is short and the area marshy and little used except for wildfowling, sailing, cruising and bird-watching. Inland, however, there are the Trent and its tributaries, draining much of the Region, and the Welland, Nene and Witham in Northamptonshire and Lincolnshire. In addition there are an extensive canal system, numerous reservoirs and many large ponds, often the result of gravel extraction. These allow much coarse fishing and some trout fishing, cruising, sailing, canoeing, rowing, water ski-ing, nature-study and walking on tow-paths and river banks. Opportunities for the use of these waters are being improved by the development of marinas such as exist at Oundle and are proposed at Colwick Park and Lincoln, by the provision of car-parks and toilets at access points, by maintenance of tow-paths and by making reservoirs available for sailing. Gravel pits at Holme Pierrepont are being developed with the aim of providing an international rowing course, while at Colwick Park it is planned to retain the racecourse and add an extensive sports centre. Sports centres and swimming pools are being provided in many places in the Region, often by co-operation between local authorities and local education authorities so that the facilities are available for schools and the general public. Access to rivers, moorland and beauty spots is being improved so that they may be enjoyed by more people, with minimum damage to amenity. Woodlands are being improved and river valleys surveyed to ensure well planned development. We commend all this action to improve the amenities of the Region, which must add to the well-being of its residents and its attractiveness to them and to the industries which the Region needs to attract or retain. In particular we applaud the arrangements for joint provision of sports facilities which permit maximum use of the facilities while keeping down the capital cost of providing them.

138. Unfortunately, many proposals for development make large demands for land. It is clear that with a rising population every acre taken from agriculture adds to the problem of feeding the population. Agricultural techniques have changed rapidly since 1939 and yields per acre have risen enormously but there can be no guarantee that the same rate of improvement will be maintained indefinitely. More land will be needed for urban purposes but it is important that the process should be regarded with a jealous and cautious eye. In particular, wherever there is a choice, and economic costs are reasonable, poor land or land which has already been affected by urban development should be taken from agriculture rather than rich and highly productive land. Differential market values may not in themselves be a fully adequate guide to these choices.

139. Some of the more immediate problems both for physical planning and long-term economic planning spring from the activities of the extractive industries.

140. The information available through the Minerals Division of the Ministry of Housing and Local Government inevitably reflects the limitations of industrial forecasting. The information available to local authorities - particularly with respect to probable demand - varies from mineral to mineral. In the case of coal - where the National Coal Board has statutory rights - demand depends on national fuel policies, which are modified from time to time. In the case of iron ore similar major national decisions are involved. In both these cases all planning must be flexible to take account of changes in world-wide factors. In the case of many other minerals - where weight or other factors reduce the scope for competition - the position is very different. In some cases there have been published forecasts of demand and even where such forecasts have in the event proved to be

underestimates, as in the case of sand and gravel, they are still much better than nothing. In other cases projections have either not been attempted or have been treated as confidential.

141. Local authorities have, of course, a direct interest in not obstructing the exploitation of their mineral wealth - it provides employment and prosperity. In any event, appeal procedure gives the central government an opportunity to weigh local difficulties against national economic needs. None the less the possibility of damage to amenity and other economic opportunity has to be taken into account, and without fuller knowledge of long-term requirements it must often be difficult for the individual local authority to reach the right conclusion on a particular case.

142. Although coal extraction is within the broad control of planning, the decision whether or not to work individual seams is not. The National Coal Board has existing authorisations in respect of large areas where there appears little likelihood of the coal being worked. The existence of the authorisations, however, causes doubts about the future stability of the land and this uncertainty can frighten off suitable development. Short-term assurances about particular sites can certainly be obtained, but long-term and interdependent physical planning over large areas must be prejudiced. Present changes in fuel policy and technology may suggest that the areas subject to this type of uncertainty could be more closely limited. Further, new decisions on exploitations may have adverse consequences on existing communities, and although local authorities can discuss these with the National Coal Board the absence of clear rights makes their intervention much more difficult.

143. Local planning authorities have power to control tipping, but this does not extend to tips which were in existence in 1947 and are still active. In this the National Coal Board is in no different position from other industries, but the consequences to the landscape are much more obvious. We welcome the consultation and voluntary agreements on the landscaping of old tips, and recognise the impossibility of imposing further financial burdens on coal extraction. None the less we do not regard as satisfactory the increasing acreage spoiled in this way, and consider that further national measures are needed.

144. Over most of the rest of the field, local authorities have planning powers; when giving consent they can impose conditions about land restoration. It is not in the interest of the communities they serve to make the operations uneconomic by imposing such conditions in all cases or making them too onerous. There is therefore a danger of inadequate restoration, due either to initial hesitation or to the subsequent bankruptcy of the companies concerned, resulting in the conditions not being fulfilled.

145. This leads on to the general problem of dereliction - which is by no means confined to mineral extraction, or to the past. The official definition of derelict land is 'land so damaged by industrial or other development that it is incapable of beneficial use without treatment.' This definition includes sites such as disused spoil heaps, worked-out mineral excavations, abandoned industrial installations and land damaged by mining subsidence; it excludes land which is still in use, e.g., active spoil heaps and refuse tips, or which is subject to planning conditions and also all dereliction arising from natural causes. At the end of 1966, the amount of derelict land in the East Midlands was 6,473 acres, 5,047 acres of which were regarded as justifying treatment. Of these 5,047 acres, 1,358 acres were in Nottinghamshire, 1,622 acres in Derbyshire (excluding High Peak) and 200 acres within the Nottingham and Derby city boundaries.

146. Dereliction excluded from the official definition often represents the major part of the problem — it includes 1,185 acres in Nottinghamshire, for instance, extra to the 1,358 acres quoted above as covered by the official definition. A cessation of working will transfer the land from one category to the other, but the problem of blight is there throughout.

147. Since land dereliction represents a wasteful use of the country's natural resources, ideally all derelict land should be rehabilitated. In the light of this probably substantial forthcoming increase in 'official' dereliction, past progress in clearance by reclamation or landscaping, whilst

Melbourne Treatment Works — Staunton Harold
Impounding Reservoir: aerial view of dam.

New Milk Marketing Board factory on Cotes Park
Industrial Estate - access to motorway on left.
This is an old colliery site, not yet completely cleared.

no doubt very welcome in the areas concerned, does not augur well for radical improvement in the environment. At 31st December, 1966 0.21% of the East Midlands was affected by dereliction as against 0.29% of England as a whole and in the two years up to that date the amount had increased by about 5% in the East Midlands and 10% in England. However, the amount in the East Midlands classified as justifying treatment had increased by 29.4% or 1,148 acres and only 174 acres had been reclaimed or landscaped. In the three years 1964-6, the percentage of land justifying treatment which was reclaimed or landscaped was 5.7% in the East Midlands, little more than half the rate for England generally. It will be noted, however, that during this period central government grants for clearance of dereliction were confined to development areas. Progress in clearance in this Region will no doubt be hastened by the 50% grant now available outside development areas; this progress will need to be kept under review.

148. Dereliction in the East Midlands ranges from making areas of poor environment worse to scarring an otherwise pleasing countryside. The National Coal Board, the Derbyshire and Nottinghamshire County Councils have all done some work in transforming stark pit heaps by recontouring prior to sowing grass and planting trees. Also advantage has been taken of opportunities to clear up dereliction when this could be achieved cheaply as a by-product of other operations, e.g., when earth was being moved for roadworks and for open-cast coal workings. Such opportunities should continue to be seized as they arise. These, together with terminal work to satisfy planning conditions and work on grant-aided schemes must be pressed forward as urgently as circumstances and financial conditions allow. Progress should shortly be reviewed to ascertain whether the administrative and financial arrangements are suitable.

149. In our view the most urgent land rehabilitation in the East Midlands is that which will reclaim sites for industry or housing, or will ameliorate dereliction where this is likely to be a deterrent to industrial development. Within these categories, first priority should in general go to the Erewash Valley so as to remove this possible deterrent to replacement industry in the areas affected by colliery closures. In particular, the Alfreton and Ripley localities and the Kirkby-in-Ashfield area all show an incidence of dereliction where the introduction of new industry needs to be encouraged. Similar considerations apply to the eastern approaches to Worksop. Although it would be possible to prepare a list of the priority order in which it would be desirable to rehabilitate derelict sites, keeping to that order would result in an overall slowing down of that programme if complications delayed progress on sites high on the list. The local authorities concerned should therefore keep their programmes as flexible as possible so that there is continuity.

150. The Council therefore considers that planning in the East Midlands requires:

(a) The safeguarding of areas where important minerals are present, so that their extraction will not be impeded, but early removal of restrictions when it becomes apparent that extraction is unlikely. In this latter respect the declining market for coal is particularly relevant.

(b) An extension of present local authority power to control dereliction.

(c) A review of the system of grants for dealing with dereliction, as early as experience of the present arrangements makes feasible.

CHAPTER 7

The next stages in regional planning

151. The Prime Minister in his statement to the House of Commons on 26th June, 1968 on the Report of the Fulton Committee said: This emphasis on regionalism will inspire our approach to some of the comments on the machinery of government which hon. Members will find in the Report. Decisions on this will be taken when the Government have received and published the reports of the Royal Commissions on Local Government.' Whilst we accept that consideration of the reports is bound to take some time, we would emphasise the need for urgency, since future changes in local government may have implications for regional organisation.

152. Whatever decisions may ultimately be reached on the pattern of regional organisation, it is important that it should have a measure of permanence. This will be essential if all the many interests and organisations which ought to contribute to regional thinking are to be encouraged to organise themselves on a regional basis and thereby maximise the regional contribution to national policy-making.

153. The general uncertainty is perhaps more apparent in the East Midlands because, more so than in other regions, the regional boundary suffers from a degree of artificiality. This is possibly reflected to some extent in governmental organisation in the region, in that the regional offices of Departments do not in all cases have comparable functions and standing with those of other regions.

154. Despite these uncertainties, some progress in creating an organisational framework for the East Midlands has been made. A Regional Advisory Committee for Further Education already existed; the Regional Sports Council which was created soon after the Economic Planning Council is showing considerable vigour; and the local planning authorities, which have statutory responsibilities for many aspects of the physical environment, have joined together to form a Regional Development Conference.

155. The most obvious lack of common organisation at the present time is in the social and cultural field. Economic planning must be directed towards a rewarding life and not merely to the creation of wealth; and even within the narrowly economic field prosperity must be largely dependent on the provision of an attractive and stimulating environment in which to live and work. We are, however, very conscious that we are not the appropriate body to deal with all aspects of environment. We are concerned rather to ensure that the Region has the institutional framework, within which environmental needs can be identified and studied, than to attempt ourselves an appreciation of the position over so wide a field.

156. Public attention has been directed of late to the problems of the immigrant communities; there is no doubt that the fact that many immigrants have a different cultural background creates difficulty, but they share, too, many of the problems of our native population. The basic trouble is that neither the physical nor the social environment of the Region provides adequate satisfaction of normal human need for large sections of the community. In this, the Region is in the same situation as the rest of our civilisation, but the frustrations not only create acute social problems, they also

act as a deterrent to economic development. In short, the Region is in need of co-ordinated advice about the social requirements of people who find the present environment unsatisfying. The appropriate organisation, to do in this field what the Regional Sports Council is doing in another, needs to be created.

157. Such an organisation would be concerned with the needs and aspirations of large sections of the community, but the importance of catering for the significant minorities must be recognised. The most obvious lack is that of an East Midlands Regional Association for the Arts, and we are glad to learn that consideration is being given to setting up such an Association. It would serve not only to bring together the various bodies within the Region interested in music, drama and the fine arts to examine how co-operation could serve the purposes common to them all, but also to provide a platform from which they could speak on level terms with other regional interests. There may well be a case for similar bodies in other cultural fields, but this will emerge more clearly if the arts, which have the advantage of precedents elsewhere, show the way.

158. The development of planning in the Region will have to take account successively of the findings of the sub-regional studies mentioned in Chapter 1. In addition two further working-groups led by the Ministry of Technology have been considering:

(a) the repercussions of a rapid expansion of computer usage in the East Midlands, and
(b) repercussions on industry generally of current developments in electronics.

The first has reported and the second is expected to report shortly. Studies, commissioned by the Council and undertaken by the universities, on retail trade patterns and office facilities will produce guide-lines for decisions of consequence to the Region. The water authorities' study of the Trent will also have a wider relevance, which must be taken into account.

159. Further work on the problems of the coalmining areas, to ensure that appropriate action can be taken in the light of the developing situation, and on the needs of the rural areas in the east of the Region is in hand.

160. Meanwhile the development of national planning, decisions on Humberside and on the pace and direction of overspill from London and other conurbations, the modifications in economic policies which may follow the report of the Hunt Committee, and developments in the transport field, will all involve progressive development and modification of planning in the East Midlands.

161. Any regional planning organisation able to assimilate and evaluate the significance of all the developments foreshadowed above will need, above all, confidence in its own continuity and the co-operation and support of bodies with primary responsibility in different aspects of regional life. We can only trust therefore, as an Economic Planning Council, that the decisions foreshadowed by the Prime Minister will be taken urgently and very explicitly in relation to regional planning.

162. Even after the necessary decisions have been taken, at no point in time will it be possible to present to the public a document as a regional plan in a final and definitive form. Planning must be a continuous process, accommodating itself to changing circumstances and, we trust, progressively improving in its own techniques and its response to public wishes. This report therefore does not pretend to do more than indicate objectives we regard as acceptable and action which would help to realise them. We are not satisfied that it presents as full and as deep a statement as we should wish and we expect in due course to report further on our conclusions, in the light of the many important reviews of national problems and policy expected during 1969.

CHAPTER 8

Summary of recommendations

163. We are strongly of the opinion that further development of the East Midlands in terms of population and of industry is both to be expected and to be desired. In order to further this development and to ensure that it is conducive to the continued welfare and prosperity of the Region's inhabitants and the nation we make the following recommendations:

IMMEDIATE ISSUES

(1)   That positive measures should be taken to replace the local employment opportunities lost in the older trades and to ensure a balanced employment structure in areas where the run-down of coalmining threatens the economic base.   (para. 20).

(2)   That the Government should recognise the Erewash Valley as an intermediate area.
                                                                                                                    (para.72).

PHYSICAL PATTERN OF REGIONAL DEVELOPMENT

(3)   That physical planning should accept as objectives desirable on economic grounds:

   (a)   The development of industry on the Alfreton-Sutton-Mansfield line.   (para. 36*(a)*).
   (b)   Continued development in the Chesterfield and Worksop areas.   (para. 36*(b)*).
   (c)   The planned expansion of south Northamptonshire.   (para. 36*(c)*).
   (d)   The development of amenity areas, particularly the traditional parklands and in the middle Trent Valley.   (paras. 26*(d)* + 137).
   (e)   The further expansion of Leicester and Loughborough.   (para. 36*(e)*).
   (f)   Small-scale development in Newark, Grantham and some other towns in Lincolnshire as a base for further expansion at a later date and in Boston to provide for better employment opportunities in the area.   (para. 36*(g)*).

(4)   That there should be a further study of the Leicestershire and south Derbyshire coalfield including its relationship with the West Midlands.   (para. 36*(f)*).

(5)   That there should be further inter-regional consideration of the potential significance of any expansion on south Humberside to Lincoln and related areas.   (para. 36*(g)*).

FACILITATION OF INDUSTRIAL MOBILITY

(6)   That industrial projects which could be steered short distances into areas with economic problems should not be denied industrial development certificates for these areas.   (para. 71).

(7)   That the criteria used by the Board of Trade to assess the needs of an area should be determined openly after discussion with Economic Planning Councils.   (para. 74).

(8)   That where an industrial move would serve a recognised social as well as a business purpose, the case for providing some public contribution towards the costs of such a move should be examined.   (para. 76).

(9)   That, after the findings of the Royal Commission on Local Government have been studied, the encouragement which local authorities could give to industrial mobility should be reviewed.   (para. 79).

(10)   That there should be adequate financial help to individuals involved in socially desirable industrial movement.   (para. 81).

ROADS

(11)   That priority should be given to:

   (a)   The Lincoln by-pass.   (para. 97).
   (b)   The dualling of A46.   (para. 97).
   (c)   The improvement of roads linking the East Midlands with Sheffield.   (para. 98).
   (d)   Improvement of A52 and A17.   (para. 99).

(12)   That the roads serving the Erewash Valley should be improved.   (para. 101).

(13)   That the local road communications of the East Midlands Airport should be improved urgently.   (para. 102).

(14)   That A6003 should be improved and A6 through Northamptonshire be replaced by a new route. Modernisation of A45 should be continued.   (paras. 103-4, 121).

(15)   That decisions to divert traffic from areas of special historic and architectural interest should not be based solely on traffic considerations.   (para. 105).

RAILWAYS

(16)   That the Nottingham-Grantham line should be retained for passenger services.   (para. 107).

(17)   That the East Lincolnshire line should be retained until satisfactory alternative passenger services have been established.   (para. 107).

URBAN TRANSPORT

(18)   That parking on major routes through urban areas should be prohibited.   (para. 109).

(19)   That further measures should be taken to stagger working and delivery hours.   (para. 110).

FREIGHT

(20)   That freight liner depots are essential in the Nottingham, Northampton and Peterborough areas, and desirable also at Leicester and Lincoln.   (para. 114)

(21)   That inland clearance depots should be established in the Nottingham and Northampton areas.   (para. 114).

(22)   That the pipeline network should be more fully exploited.   (para. 117).

AIR TRANSPORT

(23)   That the East Midlands Airport should be accepted as a developing international airport.
                                                                                                             (para. 119).

THE PHYSICAL ENVIRONMENT

(24)   That in housing development local authorities should encourage awareness of visual amenity and lead the way in preserving or improving the environment.   (para. 123).

(25)   That the public sector housing programme should be concentrated on those areas where the need is greatest.   (para. 129).

(26)   That more attention should be paid to the relationship between the price and demand for water.   (para. 134).

(27) That, if the outcome of the desk study of the Wash barrage scheme is favourable a full feasibility study should be undertaken.   (para. 135).

(28) That present reliance on flooding land for water-supply should be reviewed and, if possible, curtailed.   (para. 136).

(29) That development should, wherever possible and economically reasonable, take place on poor land or land already affected by earlier urban development.   (para. 138).

(30) That planning in the East Midlands requires:

(a) Safeguarding of areas where minerals will probably need to be extracted and freeing of areas where minerals, although present, are unlikely to be extracted.   (para. 150).

(b) An extension of present local authority power to control dereliction.   (para. 150).

(c) A review of the system of grants for dealing with dereliction as early as experience of the present arrangements makes feasible.   (para. 150).

THE DEVELOPMENT OF REGIONAL PLANNING

(31) That decisions on the future of the regional planning organisation should be taken urgently.   (paras. 151-2).

(32) That the organisation and definition of the East Midlands, within the regional planning organisation, should be reviewed.   (paras. 153-161).

(33) That an organisation be created to deal, on a regional basis, with social needs and aspirations.   (para. 156).

(34) That support be given to the establishment of a Regional Association for the Arts.
                                                                                (para. 157).

164. Many of the above recommendations are general and relate to national policies which are necessary to the implementation of regional plans. More detailed recommendations relating to particular developments must await the findings of local studies on the one hand and the further development of certain aspects of national planning on the other; some of the environmental subjects must also await the development of the appropriate institutions within the Region and the exchange of views between them. In much of this, co-operation is the key and we have every reason to believe from our experience of the last three years that in any exercise involving the public good this co-operation will be forthcoming in full measure. We conclude therefore, as we began, with confidence that the East Midlands is a Region of Opportunity.

Appendices

Migration between the East Midlands and other economic planning regions, Wales and Scotland 1965-66

APPENDIX 1

ECONOMIC PLANNING REGION	Gross movement into the East Midlands			Gross movements out of the East Midlands			Net movements		
	Total	Males	Females	Total	Males	Females	Total	Males	Females
Northern	3,940	1,990	1,950	2,700	1,390	1,310	+1,240	+600	+640
North West	6,300	3,130	3,170	5,400	2,660	2,740	+ 900	+470	+430
Yorkshire & Humberside	12,870	6,290	6,580	12,320	6,050	6,270	+ 550	+240	+310
West Midlands	9,780	4,920	4,860	8,160	4,120	4,040	+1,620	+800	+820
East Anglia	4,600	2,360	2,240	4,170	2,010	2,160	+ 430	+350	+ 80
South East	19,390	9,910	9,480	15,430	7,650	7,780	+3,960	+2,260	+1,700
South West	3,820	2,040	1,780	3,720	1,800	1,920	+ 100	+240	−140
Wales	1,950	1,130	820	1,380	750	630	+ 570	+380	+190
Scotland	4,720	2,530	2,190	2,360	1,180	1,180	+2,360	+1,350	+1,010
TOTAL	67,370	34,300	33,070	55,640	27,610	28,030	+11,730	+6,690	+5,040

Source : 1966 Census (10% Sample)

East Midlands Region: civilian population changes, 1962-67

Area	1962 Distribution		Change 1962-67								1967 Distribution	
			Total Change		By Births and Deaths		Gain to Civilian Popn. through Armed Forces run-down		Net Balance by Civilian Migration			
	'000	%	'000	%	'000	%	'000	%	'000	%	'000	%
EAST MIDLANDS REGION	3,129.8	100.0	+152.9	4.9	120.5	3.9	1.4	0.0	+31.0	+1.0	3,282.7	100.0
NOTTINGHAM/DERBYSHIRE SUB-REGION	1,688.4	53.9	+ 73.2	4.3	64.1	3.8	0.9	0.1	+ 8.2	+0.5	1,761.6	53.7
Chesterfield district	208.7	6.7	+ 9.3	4.5	7.7	3.7	0.1	0.0	+ 1.5	+0.7	218.0	6.6
Erewash Valley district	75.2	2.4	+ 0.8	1.1	1.8	2.4	0.0	0.0	− 1.0	−1.3	76.0	2.3
Derby district	330.1	10.5	+ 12.5	3.8	12.2	3.7	0.2	0.1	+ 0.1	0.0	342.6	10.4
High Derbyshire district	63.5	2.0	+ 1.2	1.9	1.1	1.7	0.0	0.0	+ 0.1	+0.2	64.7	2.0
Mansfield/Worksop district	245.2	7.8	+ 9.4	3.8	9.9	4.0	0.1	0.0	− 0.6	−0.2	254.6	7.8
Newark/Retford district	126.2	4.0	+ 10.5	8.3	5.1	4.0	0.1	0.1	+ 5.3	+4.2	136.7	4.2
Nottingham district	639.4	20.4	+ 29.5	4.6	26.5	4.1	0.3	0.0	+ 2.7	+0.4	668.9	20.4
LEICESTER SUB-REGION	663.3	21.2	+ 32.0	4.8	26.9	4.1	0.3	0.0	+ 4.8	+0.7	695.3	21.2
Leicester district	489.6	15.6	+ 21.2	4.3	21.5	4.4	0.2	0.0	− 0.5	−0.1	510.8	15.6
Leicestershire/South Derbyshire coalfield district	97.7	3.1	+ 5.1	5.2	2.7	2.8	0.0	0.0	+ 2.4	+2.5	102.8	3.1
Market Harborough district	33.9	1.1	+ 3.9	11.5	1.1	3.2	0.0	0.0	+ 2.8	+8.3	37.8	1.2
Hinckley district	42.0	1.3	+ 1.9	4.5	1.6	3.8	0.0	0.0	+ 0.3	+0.7	43.9	1.3
EASTERN LOWLANDS	373.3	11.9	+ 19.5	5.2	13.1	3.5	0.2	0.1	+ 6.2	+1.7	392.8	12.0
Lincoln district	109.5	3.5	+ 7.1	6.5	4.3	3.9	0.1	0.1	+ 2.7	+2.5	116.6	3.6
Kesteven district	102.6	3.3	+ 5.2	5.1	3.6	3.5	0.1	0.1	+ 1.5	+1.5	107.8	3.3
Holland district	103.6	3.3	+ 1.5	1.4	2.6	2.5	0.1	0.1	− 1.2	−1.2	105.1	3.2
Melton/Oakham district	57.7	1.8	+ 5.6	9.7	2.6	4.5	0.0	0.0	+ 3.0	+5.2	63.3	1.9
NORTHAMPTONSHIRE SUB-REGION	404.8	12.9	+ 28.2	7.0	16.4	4.1	0.2	0.0	+11.6	+2.9	433.0	13.2
Northampton district	152.2	4.9	+ 7.2	4.7	5.8	3.8	0.1	0.1	+ 1.3	+0.9	159.4	4.9
Kettering district	63.9	2.0	+ 1.8	2.8	1.4	2.2	0.0	0.0	+ 0.4	+0.6	65.7	2.0
Wellingborough district	97.7	3.1	+ 5.0	5.1	2.9	3.0	0.0	0.0	+ 2.1	+2.1	102.7	3.1
Corby district	38.9	1.2	+ 7.7	19.8	4.3	11.1	0.0	0.0	+ 3.4	+8.7	46.6	1.4
Daventry/Brackley district	52.1	1.7	+ 6.5	12.5	2.1	4.0	0.0	0.0	+ 4.4	+8.4	58.6	1.8

Source : Registrar General's mid-year estimates.

Note : Migration 1961-62 is excluded because of the exceptional influx of Commonwealth immigrants during that year. See East Midlands Study, Appendix 8. The 1962 total population in the Region and Chesterfield district differ from those in the East Midlands Study because of a boundary change.

57

East Midlands Region
Civilian Population:
mean annual changes by migration, 1962-67

	'000	1962-1967	%
EAST MIDLANDS REGION	+ 6.2		+ 0.20
Sub-Regions :-			
NOTTINGHAMSHIRE/DERBYSHIRE	+ 1.6		+ 0.10
Chesterfield district	+ 0.3		+ 0.14
Erewash Valley district	− 0.2		− 0.27
Derby district	+ 0.02		+ 0.01
High Derbyshire district	+ 0.02		+ 0.03
Mansfield/Worksop district	− 0.1		− 0.05
Newark/Retford district	+ 1.1		+ 0.84
Nottingham district	+ 0.5		+ 0.08
LEICESTER	+ 1.0		+ 0.14
Leicester district	− 0.1		− 0.02
Leicestershire/S. Derbyshire coalfield district	+ 0.5		+ 0.49
Market Harborough district	+ 0.6		+ 1.65
Hinckley district	+ 0.1		+ 0.14
EASTERN LOWLANDS	+ 1.2		+ 0.33
Lincoln district	+ 0.5		+ 0.49
Kesteven district	+ 0.3		+ 0.29
Holland district	− 0.2		− 0.23
Melton/Oakham district	+ 0.6		+ 1.04
NORTHAMPTONSHIRE	+ 2.3		+ 0.57
Northampton district	+ 0.3		+ 0.17
Kettering district	+ 0.1		+ 0.13
Wellingborough district	+ 0.4		+ 0.43
Corby district	+ 0.7		+ 1.75
Daventry/Brackley district	+ 0.9		+ 1.69

Source: Registrar General's mid-year estimates of civilian population. The estimates of net migration have been calculated by deducting estimates of the natural change from the total population change.

58

East Midlands Region: Home population projections, 1967-81

Thousands

Population changes 1967-71-81

Area	1967-71		1971-81		1967-81		1967	1971	1981
	Natural Change	Migration including Natural Change	Natural Change	Migration including Natural Change	Natural Change	Migration including Natural Change	Total	Total	Total
East Midlands	100	39	252	173	352	212	3,295	3,434	3,860
Sub-Regions:									
Notts./Derbys.	54	10	136	18	190	28	1,764	1,828	1,982
Leicester	22	3	57	14	79	17	695	720	791
Eastern Lowlands	10	2	26	8	36	10	402	413	447
Northants.	14	25	34	133	47	158	434	473	640

Thousands

Changes in age structure 1967-71-81

Area	1967-71					1971-81				
	Total All Ages	Persons 0-14	Males 15-64	Females 15-59	Older Persons	Total All Ages	Persons 0.14	Males 15-64	Females 15-59	Older Persons
East Midlands	139	73	16	15	35	426	158	110	108	50
Sub-Regions:										
Notts./Derbys.	64	32	7	6	18	154	56	36	32	30
Leicester	25	17	-1	—	9	71	31	15	15	9
Eastern Lowlands	11	8	—	1	2	34	15	10	10	1
Northants.	39	16	10	8	5	167	57	49	51	10

Percentage Changes in Age Structure 1967-71-81

Area	1967-71					1971-81				
	Total All Ages	Persons 0-14	Males 15-64	Females 15-59	Older Persons	Total All Ages	Persons 0.14	Males 15-64	Females 15-59	Older Persons
East Midlands	4.2	9.3	1.5	1.6	7.1	12.4	18.5	10.1	11.1	9.7
Sub-Regions:										
Notts./Derbys.	3.6	7.6	1.3	1.1	7.2	8.4	12.4	6.1	6.1	11.2
Leicester	3.6	10.4	-0.4	—	8.6	9.9	17.2	6.7	7.4	8.0
Eastern Lowlands	2.8	8.1	—	1.3	3.3	8.2	14.6	7.5	8.7	1.6
Northants.	9.0	15.6	7.0	6.5	7.3	35.3	47.1	33.0	39.1	13.6

Note: The figures are based on the 1966 Registrar General's age-sex projections to 1971 and 1981.
These incorporate 1966 assumptions of future fertility, mortality, internal and international migration, and are adjusted for
boundary changes at 1st April, 1967. For consistency, the 1981 sub-regional forecasts are controlled to the regional projections
published in the Registrar General's Quarterly Return for the 4th Quarter, 1967 (No. 467).

Employees in employment:
estimated changes in numbers between 1961-66
and range of changes forecast* for 1966-75

(thousands)

Industry Group	Estimated Numbers			Range of Changes Forecast* 1966-75	
	1961	1966	Change 1961-66	From	To
1. Agriculture, Forestry and Fishing	45.1	36.4	− 8.7	− 12.2	− 7.5
2. Mining and Quarrying	117.1	101.0	− 16.1	− 48.0	− 40.0
3. Food, Drink and Tobacco	41.9	45.6	+ 3.7	+ 0.7	+ 1.4
4. Chemicals and Allied Industries	18.3	19.7	+ 1.4	+ 0.4	+ 1.6
5. Metal Manufacture	45.1	48.1	+ 3.0	− 1.0	+ 1.0
6. Engineering and Electrical Goods	128.9	147.1	+ 18.2	+ 16.6	+ 22.7
7. Shipbuilding and Marine Engineering	≠	≠	≠	+ 0.2	+ 0.4
8. Vehicles	60.8	51.8	− 9.0	+ 1.0	+ 1.5
9. Metal Goods not elsewhere specified	18.1	22.8	+ 4.7	+ 2.3	+ 2.9
10. Textiles	119.0	124.0	+ 5.0	+ 3.2	+ 4.1
11. Leather, Leather Goods and Fur	5.0	4.8	− 0.2	− 0.8	− 0.4
12. Clothing and Footwear	87.9	77.9	− 10.0	− 8.4	− 5.9
13. Bricks, Pottery, Glass, Cement, etc.	21.2	22.5	+ 1.3	+ 0.3	+ 0.7
14. Timber, Furniture, etc.	15.4	15.7	+ 0.3	+ 0.3	+ 0.5
15. Paper, Printing and Publishing	23.7	24.8	+ 1.1	+ 0.9	+ 1.4
16. Other Manufacturing Industries	14.0	16.5	+ 2.5	+ 2.9	+ 3.9
17. Construction	81.3	95.2	+ 13.9	− 0.6	+ 1.6
18. Gas, Electricity and Water	20.3	25.2	+ 4.9	+ 5.0	+ 5.4
19. Transport and Communication	73.5	70.8	− 2.7	− 6.2	− 5.2
20. Distributive Trades	153.5	167.4	+ 13.9	+ 11.9	+ 13.9
21. Insurance, Banking and Finance	16.7	20.2	+ 3.5	+ 8.2	+ 9.2
22. Professional and Scientific Services	106.1	127.0	+ 20.9	+ 18.0	+ 23.0
23. Miscellaneous Services	79.9	96.4	+ 16.5	+ 11.6	+ 16.0
24. Public Administration and Defence	59.7	63.8	+ 4.1	+ 6.4	+ 9.6
TOTAL (rounded thousands)	1,353	1,426	+ 73	+ 13	+ 62

* The forecast employment changes 1966-75 have been based on a statistical projection of the changes observed between 1961 and 1966 modified in the light of subsequent changes and recent trends. The various factors governing future levels of employment are not readily assessable and for this reason the forecasts should not be regarded as certain estimates.

≠ The numbers are too small to be given within acceptable margins of error.

Industrial building completed for manufacturing industry only (as known at 30th June, 1968) East Midlands Region by Sub-regions

APPENDIX 6

Year Completed	Nottinghamshire/Derbyshire				Leicester			
	Projects		Estimated additional employees		Projects		Estimated additional employees	
	Number	Area '000 sq. ft.	Males	Total	Number	Area '000 sq.ft.	Males	Total
1960	78	1,500	1,330	1,720	33	474	370	560
1961	69	1,534	1,060	1,950	33	395	290	420
1962	56	1,079	700	1,410	51	727	500	650
1963	48	723	740	1,220	24	369	100	180
1964	40	618	410	800	32	427	310	450
1965	49	927	590	790	28	489	520	840
1966	53	916	480	610	27	765	660	930
1967	50	775	420	640	47	631	820	930

Year Completed	Eastern Lowlands				Northamptonshire			
	Projects		Estimated additional employees		Projects		Estimated additional employees	
	Number	Area '000 sq. ft.	Males	Total	Number	Area '000 sq. ft.	Males	Total
1960	14	177	190	500	24	480	380	560
1961	8	190	130	430	33	559	590	1,030
1962	6	134	80	80	12	157	290	330
1963	6	83	150	160	9	423	240	340
1964	10	161	60	130	18	314	390	670
1965	10	120	130	220	18	525	500	720
1966	11	275	310	410	27	396	270	450
1967	20	322	260	350	20	633	420	490

Year Completed	East Midlands Total			
	Projects		Estimated additional employees	
	Number	Area '000 sq. ft.	Males	Total
1960	149	2,631	2,280	3,340
1961	143	2,678	2,080	3,830
1962	125	2,097	1,560	2,470
1963	87	1,598	1,230	1,900
1964	100	1,520	1,170	2,040
1965	105	2,061	1,740	2,570
1966	118	2,352	1,720	2,400
1967	137	2,361	1,920	2,410

Source : Board of Trade

Projects covered by industrial development certificates - completed - East Midlands Region, 1966-1967

		Notts./ Derbys.		Leicester		Eastern Lowlands		Northants		East Midlands Total			
												Estimated Additional Employment	
		No.	Area '000 sq. ft.	No.	Area '000 sq. ft.	No.	Area '000 sq. ft.	No.	Area '000 sq. ft.	No.	Area '000 sq. ft.	Males	Total
III.	Food, drink and tobacco	6	67	5	109	2	104	3	21	16	301	180	350
IV.	Chemical and allied industries	5	65	1	10	–	–	2	17	8	92	40	40
V.	Metal manufacture	13	250	3	68	1	32	4	390	21	740	500	530
VI.	Engineering and electrical goods	18	246	25	483	7	93	7	133	57	955	1,300	1,540
VII.	Shipbuilding and marine engineering	–	–	–	–	–	–	–	–	–	–	–	–
VIII	Vehicles	7	90	5	43	2	19	5	68	19	220	380	560
IX.	Metal goods n.e.s.	11	191	3	22	3	23	–	–	17	236	130	160
X.	Textiles	18	325	9	160	2	38	–	–	29	523	250	480
XI.	Leather, leather goods and fur	–	–	–	–	–	–	4	60	4	60	–	–
XII.	Clothing and footwear	–	–	1	7	1	10	1	6	3	23	60	140
XIII.	Bricks, pottery, glass, cement, etc.	8	268	10	366	3	139	2	70	23	843	330	330
XIV.	Timber, furniture, etc.	10	105	8	57	6	84	12	194	36	440	250	310
XV.	Paper, printing and publishing	2	20	3	63	2	42	3	40	10	165	110	220
XVI.	Other manufacturing industries	5	64	1	8	2	13	4	30	12	115	110	150
	All manufacturing industries	103	1,691	74	1,396	31	597	47	1,029	255	4,713	3,640	4,810

Estimated Additional Employment

	Notts./Derbys.	Leicester	Eastern Lowlands	Northants
(Male)	900	1,480	570	690
,, Employment (Total)	1,250	1,860	760	940

Source : Board of Trade

Report of a Study Group on Textile Fibres

SUMMARY AND RECOMMENDATIONS

1. Man-made fibre production is carried on at only one location in the Region and, currently, this consists of mainly rayon and nylon. The relative proportions of the different types of fibre making up this production may change but it seems likely that fibres will be produced in the Region for the foreseeable future. Not all of the fibres go into textiles and the large proportion used to make filter-tips for cigarettes is a stabilising factor. As far as we are aware, there are no plans to introduce any new types of fibre production to Spondon. The productivity of the plant is being steadily improved and this should ensure its continued viability.

2. The knitting industry is the most important part of the textile industry in the Region. It has a bright future providing certain steps are taken. The knitting industry itself believes that with lower, 'more realistic' prices charged by the UK fibre manufacturers it could face the world with nothing to fear, but it is clear that this is not the only factor. The age of the factory buildings and the fragmentation of the industry could prove to be serious handicaps. The industry has been criticised for employing far too few production engineers. Steps are being taken to overcome these deficiencies but it is clear that a continuous policy of reinvestment in buildings and plant will be necessary to meet the foreign competition which is steadily increasing. A greater utilisation of plant, i.e., more shift working, will be necessary if these investments are to pay the proper dividends. If these policies are followed, the industry should ride happily on a boom for knitted fabrics and garments. In the very long term* there might well be a reduction in the labour requirement as further automation is achieved, but in the short term* the opposite is likely.

3. If they are to take advantage of these developments, it is clear that the textile machinery manufacturers must also move ahead as rapidly as they can. There will be developments in machine speed, pattern variations, instrumentation and control. On the making-up side welding may increasingly replace sewing, for certain applications. The limitations to the use of this technique will be steadily overcome.

4. The requirement for dyeing and finishing will continue for the foreseeable future, but it seems likely that the location of the plants will change. The small commission dyer and finisher will find it increasingly difficult to obtain sufficient orders as more and more factories install their own facilities. Once again, this is a process which is already well advanced. There will be a continuation of the efforts to reduce the labour content of this work, but the solutions to the problems are not yet in sight.

5. The Study Group is concerned at the fragmentation of two important functions of the textile industry as a whole: administration and training. The Group believes that the industry would be better served by one Training Board with sub-committees dealing with the various sections. There would then be better co-ordination of the training programmes and less confusion over the choice of Board for a particular sector.

6. The Group also would like to see the creation of a U.K. Textile Council*, which would be truly representative of the industry as a whole from fibre production and machinery construction right through to finishing. It believes that in this way a truly co-ordinated policy could be worked out and put to the Government in place of the present system of sectional groups fighting for their own interests.

---

* See comments on the following page

7.   In the field of research and development, the Study Group believes there is a need to re-examine the role of the Research Associations and Universities.* In particular, it is recommended that the Research Associations be supported by a levy ⊬ and that there should be a reduction in the number of Research Associations serving the industry.

---

* See comments below.

---

* *Comments by the East Midlands Economic Planning Council and Board*
1.   'Short term' is defined as 4 to 5 years, 'very long term' as over 20 years.
2.   In amplification of para. 6 above, there is a Textile Council in existence which is the development council for the UK cotton, man-made fibre production, man-made fibre and silk yarn processing and throwing and cloth warp knitting industries. It does not, therefore, cover the whole of the textile industry, as would the Council recommended by the Study Group, since it does not include textile machinery manufacture, the wool industry, weaving, weft knitting or all dyeing and finishing.
3.   With reference to the role of Research Associations and Universities, it should be borne in mind that the industries' Research Associations are in advance of the Universities in the field of research and development.

The introduction of a statutory levy for hosiery and knitwear research has been agreed in principle by the Board of Trade and subject to Parliamentary approval should come into effect in July, 1969.

Some Government Services to Industry

The considerable expansion in the value and variety of official services to industry in recent years may not be readily apparent to all firms who could benefit from them. These services have relevance for all areas of industry and especially for exporters. The following summary is a guide to some of the major contact points. For a completely detailed inventory of services available from any or all departments, interested firms should write to the appropriate addresses.

THE BOARD OF TRADE is the key agency providing export services through its headquarters divisions in London and through its regional offices which maintain direct links with individual firms. Each regional office has export officers always ready to help individual firms with their export problems. They undertake export promotion work in the regions similar to those carried out by the Export Services Branch of the Board of Trade in London. This branch collects and disseminates up-to-the-minute information about EXPORT OPPORTUNITIES, MARKET CONDITIONS, TARIFF AND IMPORT REGULATIONS and other essential data provided by Diplomatic Service commercial officers in over 200 British posts overseas. Other matters on which firms can get advice and positive assistance include: FINDING SUITABLE AGENTS — BUSINESS TRIPS — STATUS REPORTS ON OVERSEAS TRADERS — GETTING SAMPLES OF FOREIGN COMPETITIVE GOODS — RESOLVING COMMERCIAL DISPUTES — CALLS FOR TENDER — TRADE FAIRS AND EXHIBITIONS — BRITISH WEEKS AND STORE PROMOTIONS — ADVERTISING AND PUBLICITY — STATISTICS.

For further details of these and other specialist export services provided by the Board of Trade directly or through its grant-aided associate bodies, apply to:

Board of Trade,
Midland Regional Office,
Five Ways House,
Islington Row,
BIRMINGHAM 15.

(Tel. 021-643 8221)
(Telex 33702 - BOT BHAM)

EXPORT CREDITS GUARANTEE DEPARTMENT provides credit insurance against major financial risks incurred in overseas trading. Facilities include comprehensive policies for the normal pattern of a company's regular export business, specific policies for major overseas contracts including long credit terms of up to five years and sometimes more and related guarantees attracting Bank finance at favourable rates.

For further information apply to:

The Regional Manager,
Export Credits Guarantee Department,
Equitable House,
South Parade,
NOTTINGHAM.
NG1 2LE

(Tel. 0602 46585)

PUBLICITY FOR EXPORTS. The Central Office of Information is the government publicity agency which supplies information material and publicity services to all other government departments. Through its craft and production divisions, COI produces a daily service of information material in practically all publicity media for an audience of many millions in most parts of the world. It also serves the publicity needs of the Home departments throughout the United Kingdom.

The large majority of successful exporting firms make regular use of the COI's professional services which are freely available to any firm that can provide newsworthy material about its products or activities with an export interest.

For further information contact:

The Central Office of Information,   (Tel. 0602 46121, ext. 357)
Cranbrook House,
Cranbrook Street,
NOTTINGHAM.
NG1 1EW

MINISTRY OF TECHNOLOGY. To help improve productivity in industry by accelerating the adoption of new techniques, Mintech provides or sponsors a wide range of advisory services. Covering fields as varied as modern development and design, engineering and production technology and up-to-date management methods, the services offer technical advice, training facilities and practical assistance. These productivity services are backed by the considerable facilities and expertise of the research establishments of Mintech and the United Kingdom Atomic Energy Authority, and 43 co-operative industrial research associations.

Within the Region there are well established Industrial Liaison Centres based on colleges in Nottingham, Derby, Northampton and Leicester, helping smaller firms to solve technical problems. A mobile unit of the Production Engineering Advisory Service is available to visit firms in the Region to give on-the-spot advice and instruction on modern production techniques. Low Cost Automation Centres have been established in Leicester and Nottingham to help firms in any line of business to automate. The Regional Interlab service is providing a strong link between industrial and academic researchers and government sponsored research resources, leading to a rationalisation of research effort.

Further information can be obtained from:

Ministry of Technology,   (Tel. 0602 46121, ext. 375)
East Midlands Regional Office,   (Telex 37143 - ECONAFF NOTTM).
Cranbrook House,
Cranbrook Street,
NOTTINGHAM.
NG1 1ES

THE DEPARTMENT OF EMPLOYMENT AND PRODUCTIVITY can give advice and assistance on all employment matters. A new manpower and productivity service goes more widely than this and gives practical advice and help to achieve greater efficiency in all sectors of industry and aims at locating and removing obstacles to the more economic and productive use of resources. It covers not only the promotion of better management policies and modern techniques but also the human and industrial relations implications of problems arising from changes in technology or management control techniques.

Apart from its advisory role, the Department operates or sponsors a wide range of training services and makes grants to voluntary bodies, whose industries are not within the scope of industrial training boards, of up to 50 per cent of the cost of appointing training development officers to advise on the development of systematic training schemes within their industries.

FOR FURTHER INFORMATION, EMPLOYERS SHOULD APPLY IN THE FIRST INSTANCE TO THE EMPLOYMENT EXCHANGE FOR THEIR AREA.

H.M. FACTORY INSPECTORATE. Though primarily responsible for enforcement of the Factories Act, Inspectors are prepared to advise on all matters relating to the safety, health and welfare of workers. This can involve use of specialist engineering, construction, chemical and medical branches and the Occupational Hygiene Laboratory Service.

For further information contact:

H.M. Factory Inspectorate,   (Tel. 0602 42311)
Eastown House,
5, Lincoln Street,
NOTTINGHAM.
NG1 3DQ

Printed in England for Her Majesty's Stationery Office
by Croform Techniques Limited, London, E.C.1.
Dd. 151787 K40 5/69